Under the Cottonwood

Animal Tracks:
A Collection of Inspirational Nature Stories

by Carol Blackford

Cover artwork:

Detail of oil painting
Pa's Cottonwoods
by Stephen Randall

Painted *en plein aire* at the Ingall's Homestead in DeSmet, SD

http://stevo-distantview.blogspot.com/
https://www.facebook.com/sdpleinairsr/

Design by Cathleen Benberg

Author inquiries:
travthepaint@gmail.com

Printed in the United States of America

Dedicated to Terry

CONTENTS

Introduction

The Wisdom of a Child

I came across the remnants of a tree house years ago. It was easy to see it had not been in use for a number of years. The dilapidated structure had fallen on hard times. It looked forlorn. Harsh wind and weather had taken their toll. Bits of gray wood were strewn on the ground and only two walls remained in the tree. Still, some of the little ladder steps were intact. I was tempted to use them, but did not wish to take a chance. It was best to study it from the ground.

A lot of work and effort went into the small structure. One could see it was not simply thrown together haphazardly. At one time, small hands placed each piece together with care. More than likely a few fingers were bloodied because of an unwieldy hammer. Fragments of blue paint still clung to the door which hung precariously on a loose hinge, flapping like a torn sail. The abandoned treehouse had a story to tell. It had been a magical place that held plans, dreams and secrets.

It's a sad day when we stop climbing trees just as there is a sense of loss when a tree house falls into disrepair. Once upon a time, tree houses were the meeting places of youthful adventurers whose boisterous laughter is no longer heard. The little Robin Hoods, GI Joes and Princesses are long gone. Children grow up and find their tree houses silly or babyish. The small fort becomes neglected and ignored. It is much like the loss of innocence. Sometimes in the rush to grow up, children carelessly toss away or dismiss that which they loved most.

Do you recall discovering the blue eggs hidden in a robin's nest, or watching a butterfly escape its cocoon? Nature is an amazing classroom. When your child's heart felt the sting of betrayal of friends or family, you could always find refuge in nature's soothing arms. Confusion and anger were often replaced with empathy or forgiveness. Playing outside often dried many a tear stained cheek.

Did you ever think a salamander was a tiny dragon or wonder if a frog could turn into a prince? Sometimes books like *The Wind in the Willows* come alive with each encounter with nature. Why do garden centers sell decorations like Garden Fairies, stone statues of deer, birds, rabbits and turtles if adults did not long for them? It is a way of reconnecting to nature. Compassion, respect, patience and understanding are life lessons that nature reveals if we take time to listen. Children use their imagination. They view the world from a different perspective. Perhaps adults should do it now and again. Certainly, the world looks far different in the boughs of a mighty oak or giant cottonwood. Just ask a child. There is a sense of wonderment and joy when one is cradled in its branches. We all know the hard part is climbing back down and facing the world.

Remember the vintage *The Andy Griffith Show*? Little redheaded Opie shot a mother Robin with his slingshot. Even though he didn't intentionally mean to harm her, the accident taught a valuable life lesson about responsibility. It was heartbreaking to see him throw the lifeless bird in the air hoping she would somehow revive. Yet, it was heartening to see the chicks grow, spread their wings and fly away because of his excellent care.

We are all children at heart no matter what year we were born. We are blessed to share the earth with all of God's creatures. We will never truly know how wise they are. For they are often misunderstood. Let's hope we never become too old or cynical to build tree houses, climb trees or sit on the grass where we can learn, dream and grow.

It's not too late. Shall we begin?

THE CANTICLE
OF THE SUN

Most High, all-powerful,
all-good Lord,
All praise is Yours, all glory,
honor and blessings.
To you alone, Most High,
do they belong;
no mortal lips are worthy
to pronounce Your Name.

We praise You, Lord,
for all Your creatures,
especially for Brother Sun,
who is the day through whom
You give us light.
And he is beautiful and radiant
with great splendor,
of You Most High, he bears your likeness.

We praise You, Lord,
for Sister Moon and the stars,
in the heavens you have made them
bright, precious and fair.

We praise You, Lord,
for Brothers Wind and Air,
fair and stormy, all weather's moods,
by which You cherish
all that You have made.

We praise You, Lord,
for Sister Water,
so useful, humble, precious and pure.

We praise You, Lord, for Brother Fire,
through whom You light the night.
He is beautiful, playful, robust, and strong.

We praise You, Lord,
for Sister Earth, who sustains us
with her fruits, colored flowers, and herbs.

We praise and bless You, Lord,
and give You thanks,
and serve You in all humility.

Extract from
Canticle of the Sun
by St. Francis of Assisi

CHAPTER ONE

♠

UNDER THE COTTONWOOD

"Bambi, Quick! Faster! Faster, Bambi!
Don't look back! Keep running! Keep running!"

Bambi, a Life in the Woods
by Felix Salten, 1923

In the soft green spring, the meadowlark's song could be heard throughout the pasture celebrating life. High overhead, mysterious and beautiful hawks gathered above billowy clouds while a proud pheasant strutted his way across the field. Chip and Traveler grazed in the pasture, nibbling sweet grass after the long harsh South Dakota winter. Every now and then they lifted their handsome heads towards the boisterous dogs in the adjacent yard. Beautiful Belle, the shepherd and Peter Piper, the cheerful lab, were taking turns playing tag. Sitting a safe distance away, diminutive Callie sat on the Dutch door of the barn never leaving her post. She knew better than to get too close to the rough dogs. She was a wise calico. Besides, her job was to police the mice that foolishly entered her domain. Callie would not tolerate uninvited guests. She was a tidy housekeeper and more than earned her food and board.

Terry painstakingly painted fences while I busied myself planting flowers along the pathway. Our little house was alive that day with hard work and activity. Our place was nestled not far from Palisades State Park and Devils Gulch, famous for its Sioux quartzite shelves and stunning cliffs. The history and myth of Jesse James draw tourists every year to the Split Rock Creek which flows through the parks. Did he really make that jump? How was it possible? The question still remains. Yet, the romance of the area never disappoints. Sometimes tourists would stop and ask for directions if we were working outside. Other times truckers would honk at Traveler when he grazed close to the road. He would race away, carrying his tail held high streaming like a flag. He was younger then and enjoyed showing off for motorists. He knew he was beautiful...

The cool morning soon grew warm and sticky by early afternoon. It was time for a much deserved lunch break. Getting up from the pathway something caught the corner of my eye. I blinked and looked again. My eyes were not playing tricks. A large doe seemed to be coaxing her twins from their hiding place under a sprawling cottonwood which was close to the house. The fawns were very small and unsure of themselves. Their little white spots reminded me of *Bambi*. One was darker, almost the color of cocoa. The smaller was light golden and far more delicate from what I could detect. The doe was cautious at first, not wanting them to get too close to a human being. After a brief time, the little deer family knew they had no reason to fear that special day. I wondered. Was it the fawn's first birthday?

We quickly gathered our two happy-go-lucky dogs downstairs. They would be able to look through the walkout patio door that overlooked the field. They were good natured dogs, but we did not want to take chances. We wanted to gain the trust of the doe and her babies. We were honored she showed them off to us.

All day long the little ones nursed and played happily. We stopped our tasks and had a picnic instead. We were far enough away so it would not disturb the deer family. But, we were close enough to see the antics and affection they showed one another. Their unsteady steps eventually gave way to more confident ones. They would walk a little, look around and softly return under the trailing branches and undergrowth of their cottonwood home.

With twilight approaching, they took to their home under the sheltering bough arms of the ancient tree. We heard a soft hooting of an owl that first evening. He seemed to be a night watchman while the little family slumbered. But, in the distance the eerie howl of coyotes could also be heard. I worried about the sneaky coyotes the whole night long. I did not want harm to come to the beautiful little family that slept so soundly under the great boughs. However, that fear left as we watched each passing day the precious fawns and their graceful mother. They seemed like an extension of our family. Big Belle and Peter Piper never ventured near them, nor did they chase them, which astonished us. They were good dogs with noble hearts.

With the slow summer days, the fawns grew strong and confident. The darker, larger one seemed to be the leader. We named him Cocoa. He ran faster and wandered farther than his tiny sister, Willow. She was content to stay close to her mother and never left her side. But, from time to time the doe would seemingly scold her son when he walked too far from their home. It was fascinating to witness their movements. We would watch the scene unfold day after day between Cocoa and his mother. It was a strange and wonderful. Cocoa was bold and enjoyed his freedom. One day we did not see him in the field. Gathering binoculars, we spotted him some distance away by a small pond watching ducks. Geese and ducks would often nest in the marshy area, a favorite of hunters. Cocoa wanted to establish his independence. He was not happy in his safe little world. He was much like a rebellious child.

Every night before sunset, the little family would gather together and retire to their quiet home. When rain pelted down, lightening flashed across the open sky, and a mean, wicked wind ripped across the field, the tree kept them out of harm's way. It appeared that nature loved the deer family just as we did.

As summer days grew shorter and supper was almost ready, I heard a truck door slam with fury. Curious, I glanced out the kitchen window. Terry was racing down the gravel road. In the distance I could see angry dust clouds float up as if something was pounding hard on the rolling hills. Something was wrong! I turned the stove off, opened the door and walked fast towards the field. The deer family was nowhere in sight. I felt uneasy because they usually could be spotted in the field that time of day. I decided to take a closer look and headed out towards the massive tree. It was the first time I dared come so near. The tree had a venerable, holy presence, almost like a church. Suddenly, I felt like a trespasser and drew back. Was I welcome in this secret place? What was I hoping to find? The air was heavy and everything was still. The magnificent tree that held many secrets over its long life now knew my fears.

An hour passed. There was no sign of Terry or the deer. It was sullenly hot outside with not even a slight breeze. What could have happened? My concern grew to panic. Finally, I heard the white pickup crawl slowly down the driveway. Terry got out... "I tried to catch poachers! But, they were going so fast that I couldn't catch up! The little ones ran in the opposite direction. Their mother was the target! I saw her shot and wounded. But she ran away from the fawns!"

I wondered what went through her mother's heart

before the bullet found its mark?

My heart went numb and my eyes filled with hot tears. Then I felt rage! I grabbed my keys and took off again without thinking. Terry could not stop me. It was a fool's chase. Perhaps they went into Minnesota for we lived a mile from the border. What could I do anyway? People like that have no conscience. Who knows? They could be drunk or dangerous. I felt like a gravel banshee bent on vengeance traveling up and down rolling dirt roads. I was hoping to get a license plate, a description, anything to catch the murderers. After I came to my senses I turned around and headed home. Terry called the Game Fish and Parks with a description of the vehicle. But, the vile evil doers made their escape. Cowards are like that.

When evening darkness crept up that dismal day the orphans stood alone. They looked wistfully towards the distant creek and over the beautiful meadow. They waited for hours until it became too dark for them. They were more than likely terrified. Finally, the young ones walked under the sheltering arms of the cottonwood tree that lonely night for the first time without their mother.

Gone were the carefree days of their babyhood. In its place stood a wild world, one they would have to learn to navigate and trust. They were vulnerable. Surely, their graceful mother would reappear when it was safe again. Day after day I kept vigil as well. Common sense told me one thing, but my heart held on for her to reappear as if by magic.

As days passed, we watched as Cocoa and Willow waited for their mother. It was painful to witness. Cocoa did not stray from his sister Willow, nor did he venture far from their once safe home. I would say little prayers that the doe would miraculously show herself. But, it was wishful, illogical thinking.

For many weeks Terry would look for their mother's body in adjoining fields or lowlands. His search came up empty every time. One evening he simply said, "She must have run a long distance in panic to lead them away from her fawns." That is all he said of the incident. I could tell it hurt him to recall that ugly day. For it was a shameful and cruel act he witnessed. Why would anyone wreak havoc on the innocent?

The warmth and joy of summer were soon replaced with the crisp chill of fall. Days grew shorter. Before long, birds would take flight seeking warmer climates. The mighty cottonwood was fast losing its leaves and took on a brittle, forlorn appearance. It too could only hold on so long... When we got home from work one evening we noticed the fawns were also gone.

> *"To the attentive eye, each moment of the year has its own beauty, and in the same field, it beholds, every hour, a picture which was never seen before, and which shall never be seen again."* —Emerson

Weeks passed. Hunting season was in full gear. It felt electric with so much excitement. We often heard the sound of shotguns from all directions. Hunters searched farms fields, shelter belts and production areas. Dogs with wagging tails and sloppy, wet tongues could not contain their excitement. They were in their element, just like the hunters. Labs, yellow, black or chocolate were frequent visitors in neighboring fields. Once in a while I would spot a German shorthair, sweet faced golden retriever or Vizala. They were all loyal and fun-loving companions to their masters.

Brilliant red-golds and burnt oranges are always a lively reminder of the season. Vibrant fall is magnificent; although sad, for it bids goodbye to the season of promise. The scent of burning leaves or wood evokes fond memories of long ago days. Hot chocolate, cider and pie are flavors to savor just as pumpkins on front porches are tradition. Who does not love walking in a pumpkin patch? October seems to bring the country bumpkin out in us all. Children and adults treasure the "boo" of Halloween, trick or treat and ghost stories. I still do. But even with the fun of fall that year my heart felt hollow. I was haunted by the memory of the beautiful deer family that shared our life.

Trucks filled with happy hunters drove along gravel roads, many waving a friendly hello. I dared not look at the game their pickup held for fear of what I might see. It always tugged at my heart to see the crumpled, contorted body of a once fleet and graceful deer tossed carelessly in the bed of a truck. Sometimes it would jolt me to see a deer on top of a vehicle as proof of a hunter's prowess. Why not cover the unfortunate trophy with tarp instead of showing off? Is it necessary? I always loved Bambi eyes, big soft and luminous. My dad was a hunter just as my husband and brothers. I understand. Nevertheless, each year I feel a sense of relief when hunting season closes.

My heart that season was on the two orphaned twins. Would they be next? How would they hide from hunters? How would they survive? I prayed they would live through the long, bitter months of winter as well. Perhaps it was foolish to care so deeply. But, the little deer family shared private moments with us and I could not forget them so easily.

Throughout the frigid white winter, our two dogs played. The big field to the east sparkled like crystal when the sun hit it just right while trees took on a winter-wonderland appearance. Often tree branches looked like they had been sprinkled with powdered sugar. No wonder Belle and Piper were cheerful. Winter was breathtaking. They rolled in the fluffy snow, barking and laughing like two school kids. Wise Callie sunbathed and slept on the Dutch door on warm days. Usually one could find her burrowed deeply in the hay on cold snowy days purring. Traveler and Chip ate contentedly while winds howled fiercely outside their stalls. They were never concerned about inclement weather. They feasted on good hay, apples and carrots while Callie enjoyed her large portions of cat food. The horse's coats were very thick and fuzzy. One could mistake them for teddy bears. They knew nothing but love. Of course, they were not wild creatures who had nobody to feed them or keep them safe. And so, I would often reflect on the vulnerable ones, Cocoa and little Willow through the long winter.

When spring arrived it was a welcome change as it always is. The earth was alive once again. Gentle rains came, the sun warmed the old earth, and robins bounced in the grass happily looking for worms. Their cheery songs gave hope. Little bird's nests were hidden in trees as well as our tiny barn. Everything was new and fresh. Life held promise for all living things. It was the gentle season of soft green grass and yellow daffodils.

It was in May, that a precious sight unfolded before our eyes. The sun was setting on what had been a perfect spring day. It cast a soft pink hue across the back pasture. Everything seemed to have a gentle glow that evening. A robin's song could be heard in the old cottonwood before settling in for the night. It was blissful. Just as we were closing the screen back door, we noticed four deer along the fence line. We quietly closed the door and stepped back outside to catch a glimpse. They were stunning... So powerful was the scene that Terry and

I still question what we saw.

Two deer appeared to be full of merriment. They ran back and forth from one another. The other two just stood in quiet dignity off to the side. It was an unusual scene and we were captivated. We witnessed what appeared to be some sort of dancing or prancing under the weary old cottonwood tree. Terry looked astonished. We glanced back and forth to one another as if we both could not believe what was happening. The two lively deer walked closer and closer to us! One was a dark cocoa color and the other a light golden shade with delicate refined features. The delicate doe had eyes the color of caramel. The larger one, a young buck had darker eyes, a little fierce. Terry and I looked at one another and knew they were the twins. Slowly, they walked back to the huge cottonwood. They seemed to be inspecting the area. Every now and then they would lower their heads or lift them high. We had no idea what they were doing. Their two companions, another doe and buck, never approached the tree. Instead, they remained close to the fence line, not far from us, as if standing guard. We all watched as Willow and Cocoa lingered around their babyhood sanctuary. It was a poignant and rare sight.

Then with great dignity, the twins walked quietly away from the sheltering tree towards us. We did not make a sound. Traveler and Chip stood as if in a trance. They did not nicker. For once the dogs were silent, even reserved. I was proud of their restraint.

Perhaps we were all awe struck. It is a mystery to this day why the dogs did not bark or even attempt to chase the deer. Why didn't the horses run with excitement either? But, we were grateful to them. We all stood frozen while the twins glanced a few moments to the east and back to us as if to say thank you for loving us old neighbors. They were right, we did love them.

We watched in awe as Cocoa and Willow flew across the field with their friends. Terry and I will never forget the scene. The moment was unforgettable. We both were completely transfixed by what took place. For one can't easily dismiss such a moment in nature, nor underestimate God's creatures.

As the years passed, we never caught a glimpse of Cocoa or Willow nor did the ancient tree shelter another deer family. In time, we too moved away. But, we left a little piece of our hearts behind. Sometime later, Terry told me the doe's body was found two miles away in a corn field by a farmer. The Game Fish and Parks also caught the poachers. Yet, it could not erase what they had stolen from the twins or us.

A Dog's Soul

Every dog must have a soul,
somewhere deep inside
Where all his hurts and grievances
are buried with his pride.
Where he decides the good and bad,
the wrong way from the right,
And where his judgement carefully
is hidden from our sight.

A dog must have a secret place,
where every thought abides,
A sort of close acquaintance
that he trusts in and confides.

And when accused unjustly
for himself, He cannot speak,
Rebuked, He finds within his soul,
the comfort he must seek.

He'll love, tho' he is unloved,
and he'll serve tho' badly used,
And one kind word will wipe away
the times when he's abused.
Altho' his heart may break in two,
his love will still be whole,
Because God gave to every dog
an understanding Soul!

— *Author Unknown*

Chapter Two

✿

Little River

It all began after the untimely death of Bach. Bach was a stunningly good looking black/red German shepherd. He was proud and highly intelligent. Now, he was gone. My heart ached to hug him and pet his soft head. I missed our long walks where we would "discuss" life. He was special no doubt. He was a big fellow, proud and true. Yes, a dog can steal your heart with their soft brown eyes and non-stop affection. Sometimes a pet can be a best friend and confidant when human company just won't do. We bond with them because they don't judge us. It is a simple uncomplicated relationship which to me is the best kind. A dog is honest and faithful.

A year passed before I trusted my heart enough to bring home another puppy. My husband and I felt it would help us both heal. We wanted to find one with good traits, stable personality, sociable, intelligent and pretty. In short, we wanted another Bach.

It felt like an adventure that sunny day in late May. For no matter how old one is, picking out a new puppy is a wonderful experience. By the time we pulled into the breeder's farmyard I was giddy.

We were met by someone who looked like Santa Claus in bib overalls. The farmhouse resembled an issue of *Country Living* and exuded antique charm. Mrs. Claus was warm and kind. She made us feel welcome. We were off to a good start. Yet, I could not help but wonder why there were so many dogs.

Terry and I looked at quite a few beautiful puppies that afternoon. We wanted to take our time with such a big decision. After all, they share our lives and homes for many years. It was amazing and delightful holding so many puppies and observing them. Some were shy, others aggressive. Did we want a female or a male pup? Did we want a tan/black or a red/black like Bach was? Finally, we found the perfect puppy. He was a friendly little guy just eight weeks old. He was playful yet not feisty. I could tell he would enjoy obedience class. I thought we would bond through daily lessons. His black/tan markings were stunning and his eyes almost a forest green. I was taken with his eyes because they seemed to look right through me. I knew they would eventually turn dark brown. He had sturdy legs like tree stumps and huge paws like mitts. But what impressed us most was the way he carried himself. He was filled with confidence and enjoyed following us. I fell in love when his little pink tongue caressed my cheek. He was going to his forever home that day.

On the return home it occurred to me that our puppy needed a name. Much thought went into the decision. We tossed names back and forth. Let's see. As a puppy Bach loved listening to classical music on the radio. He would fall asleep when he heard Bach. He did not respond well to country music or he would have ended up Hank. The classical sounds soothed him. Then I remembered my little dirty buckskin horse named Timber. His color was rugged. He made one think of Colorado or Montana. My mind searched and then it came to me, why not River? A river is majestic and mighty. The pup will be a big dog someday. So, our beautiful puppy with deep forest green eyes was named River. It was a perfect fit.

Now, there was one more thing I forgot to mention, old Thor. Old Thor was Terry's hunting buddy. He was thirteen years old suffering with poor eyesight and considerable arthritis. He was often in constant pain and sometimes walked on three legs. Our vet prescribed pain medication which helped ease his suffering. Sadly, we often found no amount of pain medicine could relieve him. He once could leap into the back end of a pickup and maneuver through fences on hunts. But, at this stage Terry had to pick Thor up and gently place him in the truck. I noticed Thor almost seemed mortified. It hurt us to see him a frail senior citizen instead of the robust dog he once was. We still remembered a plush coated yellow lab with endless energy and a massive appetite. He was prone to plump and was as obstinate as a mule. He could be a clown too. I never understood why he preferred lounging in mud instead of grass. However, he really reminded me of a grumpy old gnome. Thor had his own peculiar personality. Yet, he was a born hunter and Terry's buddy. He loved Terry and had no time for anyone else. For the dog and I shared Terry one could say. To this day the mere mention of Thor brings Terry to tears. Those two had an unbreakable bond.

Introducing the two dogs would not be easy. I was concerned for River. What if old Thor would wish to harm him? What if Thor felt unloved or unwanted? This would take time and patience. For animals, like people, can be jealous and lash out.

As soon as old Thor spotted River in my arms he let out a low growl. It was not a good sign. Terry said, "Put the pup down. Thor will not hurt him." I was not so sure and did not want to take a chance. It took some coaxing on Terry's part for me to be convinced. I was fiercely protective. Finally, I released River. He ran straight to old Thor and licked his ancient white whiskered face. Thor immediately stopped growling. He allowed the clumsy puppy to roll and crawl all over him. He even seemed to enjoy it. Thor behaved with patience and benevolence. My worst fears were over. We had a built in babysitter with the cantankerous old dog. Recalling the incident, I think it made Thor feel needed and important once again. The two dogs became inseparable.

A few days passed when we noticed something unusual. When River ate his food he would hiccup. At first we thought nothing of it. But, after the second day I called a vet to check River. She examined him and found him to be a beautiful, healthy puppy. I was relieved but not convinced. If nothing was wrong why was he always hiccupping? He even started to throw up his food. I made an appointment with another vet. It was time for a second opinion.

It was a long wait in the vet's office. My daughter Tara accompanied me which helped the time pass. But, I could see she felt concern too. I thought it was a routine checkup. What was happening? The vet ran numerous tests on River. Was it necessary? He was such a loving puppy and never once whimpered. He was a brave little soldier through it all. I knew something was wrong when the vet asked me into her office. There she showed me the results of the x-rays and tests. River was born with a birth defect called Mega Esophagus. In other words, it was a death sentence.

No words can describe how hollow I felt. The vet explained in fine detail the dire condition River was faced with. Softly she said, "It is time to put him to sleep." I respected her professional advice. But, I was not ready to say goodbye, not yet. We had plans the two of us, after all. I looked straight in the kind vet's eyes, choking back tears and said, "I will give him the best two weeks any pup could possibly have. When the two weeks are up, we will then say goodbye to River, but not before".

And so, we took River home where we would lavish affection on him. His meals were the difficult part. His beautiful little head had to be held up so he could swallow. It was a slow, sad process. But, we managed to see he was well nourished and content.

What made River beautiful was his playful, delightful nature. He seemed to ignore his grave condition. He romped with Grandpa Thor and ran as fast as his baby legs could take him. He would push his little nose up to the fence and touch noses with the two horses, Traveler and Chip. He was fearless, curious and wonderful. Yet, I wondered if he knew his time was brief and simply wanted to explore the world?

One day while watering flowers I felt a tug on the water hose. I looked around. It was beautiful River trying his best to pull it away from me. I let go and watched him grapple with the unwieldy hose. In fact, so did old Grandpa Thor. It was the first time Thor let go of anything. He always stubbornly refused to give in, but he did that day. Did Thor know too?

River loved flowers. The first day we brought him home he plunked down in my flower bed and began sniffing the blossoms. When he grew weaker I would cradle him with sweet smelling blossoms. His small face grew thin and he looked like a frightened fox instead of a shepherd. I knew it was time to say goodbye; but, I still refused to say goodbye to my Little River. River was now called Little River because he would not have a chance to grow mighty. Yet, little rivers run deep just like the love we had for him. Our pets are funny that way. They nestle in our hearts and take root.

I raced home from teaching class one day to find nobody home except Thor. I searched for a note, but found nothing. I knew. Terry took Little River to the vet hospital without me. I was angry and mystified. Why would he do such a thing? Then I realized he was sparing me more anguish. I broke down and wept.

A few hours passed. Finally, Terry pulled up, got out of his pickup and was carrying what looked like a beautiful mahogany box. It was a tiny masterpiece. I knew he had been working on something, but he did not tell me what it was. It was his way. I could see he was downcast from the way he walked with his head down. He usually smiles but not this time. He came close and placed the polished wooden box in my arms. I opened the tiny coffin that Terry made for the pup. Inside Little River appeared to be sleeping on a soft red velvet fabric. I buried my nose into his soft baby fur and kissed him for the last time. Goodbye, my Little River...

We carried our Little River into a small meadow area close to the pasture. I placed a statue of a sleeping angel on his grave that I chose especially for him. His tiny grave was close to a young spruce tree Terry planted. We both felt crushed and did not speak. Terry walked back to the house, but I lingered for a while.

Two weeks passed and we noticed Thor was limping more than usual. It was obvious he felt worse. He acted depressed as well. When Thor stopped enjoying food it was a very bad sign. For no matter what befell Thor, he loved meals.

When the horse vet came out the next day to inoculate Traveler and Chip, we asked him to examine Thor too. He shook his head and said the old dog was in great pain and no pills could help. He only had the use of three legs as well. It was cruel to allow him to go on. Terry looked at me, and just shook his head.

And so they were once again side by side in the little meadow where they once explored. Terry put Thor in a small hunting jacket with his collars and leash. We lined his grave with a soft sheet and gently placed him alongside Little River. I put a small carved wood duck on Thor's grave as he was a great hunter and fine grandpa to Little River. Then, I sprinkled thousands of wild flower seeds on both graves so each spring the meadow would look joyful for years to come and ever on.

The next three nights we looked out to see our small meadow flooded with fire flies. It was so lively and bright it resembled thousands of twinkling Christmas lights! It was a celebration and we knew they were together.

CHAPTER THREE

❀

GENTLE BELLE

The dimensions of Belle's world were 42" x 27" x 29". The big beautiful dog knew little else other than her cramped crate. She was a prisoner. Day after day she languished until she lost weight and her once thick and luxurious coat became dull. A TV was left on in hope it would assuage her anxiousness, but it was only a sound with images that meant nothing. The constant tick-tock of the living room clock became annoying. Her nervous energy was spent grooming and licking her fur until bald patches appeared. Her only companions were boredom and loneliness. Her exquisite almond eyes took on a broken look. Her 110 pound weight dropped to a mere seventy pounds. She appeared to look more like a greyhound instead of a German shepherd dog. One could see her ribs show. Little by little her lively spirit was being crushed.

It wasn't always that way. At one time she lived

in a house with a big yard to play in. Her heart longed to roll in the grass or chase a Frisbee. Sometimes her people would go to a lake or camp out. How she enjoyed the outdoors. One night she watched as an owl perched in a tree over the tent. The bonfire was bright and the humans sang songs. She remembered tasting hot dogs and sneaking a bite of a marshmallow her people shared with her. In those days Belle felt important as she protected her family from would-be intruders—human or animal. In short, big Belle loved being needed. She was a kind, obedient and gentle giant of a dog. Rarely did she growl or bark. It was a glorious time and she felt beloved.

That was before her owners broke up. The tell-tale signs were apparent to the dog. Harsh words and cold glances were all too common between the man and woman, her people. What happened to the love? Gone were the tender caresses and sweet words of endearment. In its place were accusations and bitterness. For the dog did not understand, being a dog. All she knew was something dark and cruel destroyed the happy world of her puppyhood. Before long, the house was sold and everything divided between the couple. Belle was caught in the middle—having loved both. She would run from the man to the woman with her tag wagging thinking somehow it would mend what was broken. Sometimes she would drop her toys at their feet, hoping the shouting would stop. She soon found nothing would help. The marriage died. And so it was decided that Belle remain in the custody of the woman.

Now, the woman was not a cruel person. She truly cared deeply for her dog in the beginning. She handpicked Belle out of the litter and brought her home. Not once was Belle mistreated by her people. But, one does not need to be physically abusive in order to mistreat a pet. The woman never intended to neglect beautiful Belle. But, her depression ate her up. The highlight of the dog's day was hearing the door unlock and seeing the woman. Perhaps they could go for a walk or take a ride in the car? More often than not the woman would drag herself in from her job. She would open the crate, put Belle on a leash, and walk her to the common area of the apartment building just long enough to relieve herself. The dog had little time for more. Gentle Belle had few requests. She only wanted affection, clean water, food, love and time to play. Tragically, Belle simply was forgotten in the turmoil and heartbreak of divorce. She was a victim and had no voice.

It took almost a year for the woman to realize that Belle was suffering. She stubbornly held on to Belle in the tiny apartment. It was too much for her to bear losing the beautiful big dog after losing her husband. Belle seemed to be a symbol of a broken dream. Finally, the woman gave way to what was best for Belle after the urging of friends and family members. It was time to give up the sweet dog for adoption. She would have a second chance and finally escape her tiny cell.

At the same time hundreds of miles away, we discussed a little journey.

"What makes you so certain this is a good idea? It's too soon don't you think? I don't want to get hurt again!" I remember saying. I recalled an especially poignant poem titled *The Power of the Dog* by Rudyard Kipling. It always left me with a lump in my throat.

I was still mourning the loss of my precious puppy Little River and resented the insinuation that a new dog could somehow take his place. Of course, we all know a new pet can't possibly take the place of another nor should they be expected to. But, we can build new memories just the same. The question was whether or not I was up to it. Who needs more heartache? Just ask anyone who has lost a beloved pet. The wound is deep. Once a bond is established with a pet there is no going back. Give your heart to a dog and they will give theirs back.

"Heaven is the place where all the dogs you've ever loved come to greet you" the saying crossed my mind because of its comforting message. Pet lovers need to remember such quotes.

A well-intentioned vet shared our loss with a dog adoption program in Iowa. She saw our anguish and tears. Her kind concern proved healing. So, I listened closely when her vet tech explained the purpose and goals of the dog adoption program. It was a worthwhile and touching program that benefited both the unfortunate dogs as well as their new owners. I finally gave in despite my initial reluctance. After all, I was adopted. Adoption works for children—why not animals?

One afternoon the phone rang with a possible match. My husband was enthusiastic about the possibilities. The Dog Rescue & Adoption person described the match as a tall female German shepherd around four years old. She had the typical black/tan saddle, a gorgeous face and an engaging personality. Now, I was intrigued. Perhaps taking a peek wouldn't hurt I thought to myself.

"Remember, nobody said we have to take the dog home. If it doesn't work we are under no obligation. Let's at least take a look. Besides, it will be a fun day trip. Give it a chance. What do we have to lose?" my well-meaning husband said.

The following Saturday we took the three-hour journey to see the dog. As luck would have it, the day proved beautiful. Was it a good sign?

We arrived midafternoon. The quaint farmstead was hidden behind tall trees. The yard had toys strewn about, a wading pool and laughing children. Some were playing fetch with dogs. There were terriers, mixed breeds, labs, and even toy dogs looking like they were having the time of their lives. A few came up to us good naturedly, tails wagging, and tongues lolling, hoping we would join in on the fun. However, we did not see the German shepherd amongst the little group.

A screen door opened and a pretty woman stepped out. She greeted us with a handshake and asked how our drive was. I got the impression we were being assessed. In a sense, we were.

After our visit she took us towards a weathered red barn in the back. Suddenly, we saw a very tall, very thin dog running alongside a man. It was the German shepherd. She saw us and immediately ran up as if she had known us her entire life. I was taken aback by her enthusiasm. She seemed to gravitate to my husband immediately. Oh, she liked men one could see that. That made me chuckle. Was she a flirt?

When she came up to me I was taken by her spectacular eyes. They were gorgeous and filled with intense intelligence. They were a sort of caramel color and reminded me of something out of ancient Egypt in shape and framed by black eyeliner. For her face bore a resemblance to one of the exotic mysterious faces one sees in Art History books. She was stunning.

Yet, she was painfully thin! Her ribs showed and her coat looked lackluster. We also noticed her determination to keep up with another, larger dog. She had a proud spirit one could see. She did not want to appear subservient to the larger male dog. I respected that greatly. She had dignity and did not wish to cower. She carried herself well.

By this time my husband was tossing a Frisbee for her. She loved it! I could tell he liked her a lot.

But, what dog doesn't like to play I thought. That is all well and good. But, an obedient, intelligent dog means a great deal more. I wanted to spend time with her too. We needed to become acquainted.

"What is this pretty girl's name?" I asked.

"Her name is Belle" the man replied.

"Belle, huh? I love that name, it suits her," I replied.

"Belle, come!" I called out. Let's see if she can break away from the fun, I thought.

Immediately she turned her head. She came running and sat down directly in front of me. It was apparent somebody taught her a few things.

"Do you have a leash I could use?" I asked.

I placed the leash on her collar, moved her gently to my left side and took a few steps. Belle followed slowly, never once pulling on the leash. I then picked up the pace a little more and said "Belle, heel!" She kept pace with me, sometimes looking into my eyes. She was a special one. She only wanted to please and it touched my heart. I had an urge to hug her tightly.

My husband glanced at me when I took the leash off. We were thinking the same thing. Belle was a keeper.

Before we could discuss the adoption fees, gather the paperwork and get things in order, Belle disappeared. We looked around and called her name. What in the world… The children told us she ran past them while we stood talking to the young couple.

"What direction did she go?" I asked. They pointed towards our pickup. We had the tail gate down and topper up. Belle already jumped in the back and was patiently waiting. It was obvious she felt the same way we did and was ready for her new home.

Over the course of a month Belle's appetite improved and she gained much needed weight. I enjoyed watching her chow down on the vet recommended products. Of course, she also had her dog treats! Her thick coat was shiny and soft. One could see she was extremely happy. It looked like she had a permanent smile tattooed on her face. She was sunshine 24/7. Pretty Belle loved nothing more than stretching her long limbs in the grass or roaming the pasture. Her crate days were over! Her bed was on the couch in the downstairs family room. It sat in front of the patio door where she could look at the endless fields.

She also loved taking rides, especially in a pickup. We had a topper and bed liner for her safety. She possessed exquisite manners while driving in the backseat of my car too. I would put a blanket down and she would prop herself up in a dignified manner. She never tried to hop in the front seat like some dogs do. Belle sometimes acted as if I were her chauffeur.

Now Belle had a soft heart for children. She

treated them with great affection and patience. She loved to be loved and to give love in return. Our granddaughters were treated gently at all times. She never snapped, growled or showed her teeth. She would roll over so one could rub her tummy, or put her large, soft head on our laps. She was always happy to shake hands. I guess she felt it was expected of her to extend her paw. People would always come up and say "I love Belle!" or "how is Belle?"

My husband was right, she did help mend my broken heart. Adopting her was a blessing.

Over the years Belle surprised us in many ways. She liked to golf! Yes, she loved golf. We had a little area to practice golf. The tiny course had three tee boxes and two holes. Belle would stand to the side and walk alongside us while we golfed—a canine caddy. Once the ball was in the cup she would wait, pick the ball out and bring it to us. If a person wanted to practice their drive Belle would retrieve the ball. She was amazing and took pride in her little job.

One of her other talents was retrieving. A German shepherd is not known to be a hunting dog. But, for some reason Belle felt it was her duty to take on the role of Labrador retriever. When my husband would put on his hunting jacket, boots and cap it was her signal to go to work. She had the desire to please no questions asked. Yes, retrieving is best left to those special canines bred specifically for it. But, just try telling Belle. Each time he left her at home to go hunting she looked dejected. I would coax her with special treats or take her outside to do yard work. However, gardening did not amuse her. She would only mope or look bored. Sometimes she would try to herd Traveler like a sheep. One day he grew impatient with her pestering, turned and ran straight for her! She was terrified and never tried to herd him again. One thing about Belle, she was a quick study and knew her limitations with the horse.

Because her heart was so sweet, I renamed her Gentle Belle. Perhaps that is why she never became a police dog. She never met a person she did not like. Belle was a constant joy and a source of pride. A good dog is a special kind of angel. Their love is unconditional and nonstop.

When Belle turned eight I enrolled her in a local obedience school. As a young woman I took my other dogs to the Kennel Club for training. They always seemed to do quite well. Therefore, obedience school only made sense. A well behaved dog is welcomed by most people. But, an unruly, ill-mannered or timid dog can be a liability. They cause problems from possible dog bites to mounting insurance premiums. Why take a chance? So, it would be no more than a little refresher course for Gentle Belle. Besides, it is fun to teach an old dog a few new tricks now and then.

By this time, we noticed Belle was experiencing trouble with her hind legs. Tragically, she had the onset of arthritis. The vet prescribed a low dose of pain medication which helped alleviate much of it, at least for a while... So, training would be just fine and would not cause her discomfort. You see, by this time both Gentle Belle and I shared something in common: arthritis. Mine came first.

When Belle saw me limp or stumble, she always waited. Her beautiful, knowing eyes were filled with love and I knew she understood my pain. We had each other's backs. When I limped, Belle limped. When she cried with pain I would hug her ever so gently to reassure her. On more than one occasion she would take my hand in her mouth and place it on her back. At first I had no idea what she was trying to convey. She was trying to get me to lean on her for balance. Yet, she was in great pain herself.

Dogs can be surprisingly selfless and she proved it. However, to do such a thing was unthinkable. It was much better if we walked slowly together and touched one another gently... a cane was meant for support, not a beloved pet. Her carefree leaping days were done. So, my husband would lift her gently in his arms and place her in the passenger side of the pickup. For Belle still loved to go down gravel roads and look at the fields, livestock and countryside. She was a bit of a cloud watcher too—a little bit of a dreamer.

As it turns out, Gentle Belle won two awards for her obedience. She was a brilliant dog scholar. Sometimes she would look at the younger pupils with disdain. It was really funny to see her glance at some of the antics the ill-mannered dogs put their masters through. It was often embarrassing to witness at times. Belle remained dignified and aloof. I was so proud of her demeanor. She never acted weird or rude. Certainly some of the other dogs were quite beautiful, but they were not very bright. At times Gentle Belle just looked at me with a glint in her eye as if to say these pups will never amount to anything. I honestly believe she read my mind!

Over the course of a few years, our Gentle Belle suffered with eye problems too. It grieved us to see her once sparkling and unusual eyes grow dim. It broke our hearts to see her whimper and suffer with arthritis. Yet, her tail always wagged and she always wanted to be cuddled.

As if her pain wasn't bad enough, we were told she would also go blind soon in not one, but both eyes. She inherited a congenital eye disorder as well as hip dysplasia. Our hearts were broken. Belle was not even ten years old. We knew what was next...

Our beautiful Gentle Belle died one bright November day. We buried her next to one of our little homemade golf greens, along the fence line. She loved to look at the rabbits hop back and forth between the shelterbelt. We never once saw Belle chase one. She simply watched them in amusement like so many things.

Now she is at rest, just a few yards from us—her people. She is our last dog. I knew she would be. A small memorial rock with a poignant saying became her tombstone, along with a sweet angel statue holding Gentle Belle's golf ball.

Chapter Four

❖

Gauge

Gauge could be considered a pretty boy. He was a downy-soft ivory colored lab pup. He had enormous paws and a great square chin. He was a dream pup. His features bespoke a gentle and playful nature. Large brown eyes were highlighted with natural charcoal-black eyeliner. In fact, he actually looked like he wore eye makeup. Of course, he was still a Labrador not a stuffed toy. In time he would be expected to accompany his master and hunt waterfowl and game birds.

Now, Gauge did not get treated like an ordinary puppy from what we determined. He had been held back while his litter mates were sold because he was so adorable. He was truly the pick of the litter. He was given run of a beautiful house, held, rocked and pampered like an indulged only child. I smiled as the owner held him close, cooing to him. She gave him a whimsical name too. I understood her affection. The roly-poly pup was too cute for words. However, my husband cringed when he heard the dainty name. Perhaps it was a sign of things to come?

After an hour passed, we were interviewed by the couple who advertised their fine puppies. They needed proof we would provide a stable, loving home for their little darling. "Will he have a big yard? Is it fenced in? Who is your vet? Will you have time to train him? Will he be neutered? If not, you must sign these papers." It felt a little like an inquisition not a transaction. However, I was impressed with the couple and had questions of my own. Yes, we all felt satisfied that the gorgeous white bundle would find a perfect home with us.

My husband was an avid hunter. He enjoyed having a well-trained hunting dog to retrieve water fowl or game birds. He would spend long hours training his hunting companions. It was important to have a dog that could be trusted to obey commands, retrieve and show good manners to other hunters as well. I remember how Thor started his training with a clothes pin. He was tiny and a wooden clothes pin was a perfect match for his little mouth. The ivory pup would be renamed Gauge and his basic training would start immediately.

Well, I bought the ivory colored puppy for my husband after his old buddy Thor died. Thor was amazing in the field and water. One could call him a natural. He was a bright pupil and always attentive. He had grit. Thor was like a miniature tank. He refused to stop. We often wondered why he never seemed to grow weary. Like the Energizer Bunny, he kept going on and on and on... For some reason I thought all labs would take naturally to water and hunting. It shows how little I knew. To my way of thinking why not find an extraordinarily beautiful one too? That way I could have a gorgeous dog and my husband could have a hunting buddy. It all made sense, right?

Gauge proved to be a sweet dog with good manners which I appreciated. One could see he was not going to be a problem dog in the house. He never had accidents and he never showed signs of aggression or barked. I was thrilled with his good nature, refined house manners and beauty. Big Belle treated him like he was her own pup. She doted on him. Belle never had pups of her own. We wondered if Baby Gauge and Belle would get along. Instead of rivalry she took him under her wing. Belle indulged the puppy always. She was his bodyguard too, as we found out.

"Blown out of the prairie and dew,
Half bold and half timid, yet lazy all through,
Loath ever to leave, and yet fearful to stay,
He limps in the clearing, and outcast in gray."
Coyotes by Bret Hart (1836-1902)

Tall grass, bushes and trees grew along the fence line which naturally dropped into a ditch. It was impossible to mow given the terrain and rugged fencing. Meadowlarks, rabbits and pheasants could be spotted in the deep overgrowth. Our large 1880s horse drawn wagon sat adjacent to the little ditch and fence line as well. Basically, it was a perfect hiding place.

Over the summer we had pesky coyotes come down from their little hill and close to our home. During the daylight hours they knew their boundaries. However, once the sun set it was a whole different dynamic. Night after night their strange cries could be heard coming closer and closer to our house. We would get up in the wee hours to see groups running in the pasture, field or by our tiny barn. Coyotes can be more than a nuisance. They are predators—unwelcome visitors.

In the daytime we looked at them through binoculars. A few times they would peer with a laser intensity right back in a bold, defiant manner. We sensed they were planning something. Coyotes are tricksters, no doubt about it. They are great survivalists too. For some reason our place caught their attention. What could it be?

We heard stories about unsuspecting dogs being coaxed by coyotes. One farmer told me a dog will be lured by a coyote for whatever reason, possibly to mate only to discover a very different fate. Could it be true I wondered? I guess anything is possible in nature.

I remember hearing cicadas and crickets one afternoon when we heard frantic yelping. It was little Gauge. His terrified cries interrupted their chorus. What was going on? I called for Belle and the foolish puppy. No answer. My husband and I ran to the other side of the house and saw fat little Gauge between Belle and a large coyote. When the coyote saw us it quickly turned and ran.

"That is a huge coyote. He's as big as Belle!" I heard myself say.

"That's not good!" my husband replied.

The farmer's words haunted me. What if our beloved dog was being somehow lured to her fate? I was hysterical with worry when we spotted her in the distance still on the heels of the huge coyote. Desperate, we grabbed the foolish pup and got into our truck to rescue Belle. Before we got out of the driveway we spotted Belle with triumph written all over her demeanor. She was exhausted. Her tongue was hanging to one side and she had cockleburs in her pretty fur. But, she was unscathed, thank heaven. At that moment we knew Belle had saved Gauge from being the main course for a hungry coyote. She was ever vigilant. If not for her he would have been murdered. The coyote had a perfect hiding spot and in broad daylight. We had no idea how long he spied on the fat puppy playing. But, he had no idea how courageous big Belle was either.

Over the course of a year, Gauge grew into a stunningly handsome Labrador. He was a lover though, not a hunter. Time and time again my husband would take him into the field behind our pasture for lessons. All would go well until he heard the sound of gunfire. As soon as the gun would fire, he would run back to the house and cling to my side. This went on for quite some time. He would stand politely with my husband and bolt back to the house when the gun would fire. Now, Terry is a patient man, but he finally gave up on Gauge being a hunting dog. He did not have a hunting companion in Gauge but we did have another gentle, good natured dog nevertheless. For some reason we felt Gauge was meant to be much more than a lap dog.

Every now and then we would chat with a neighbor who lived two miles south of us. She would walk by our home on a daily basis. One day she mentioned a young widow and her sons that were going through a particularly difficult time with the recent loss of their father and husband. As anybody knows, the death of a loved one is never easy. But, unexpected death can be especially jolting. Unless someone has suffered such loss, it is hard to fully understand the depth of their loss. Everyone grieves in their own way and in their own time. How does one have the strength to be both mother and father when they need to nurture their own broken heart?

One evening my husband and I were at the home of some friends that lived in the same neighborhood as the widow and her boys. Before we left they shared their concerns for the family. They explained to us how quiet the sons were since the loss of their daddy. They were still in a state of shock which is understandable. Nothing is ever the same when a parent dies. Our hearts felt heavy after hearing the story once again. How tragic for the mother and her little boys.

When we left the couple's home we glanced across the street where the widow and her boys lived. It was a nice home with a huge yard. It seemed empty and quiet however. The shades were drawn and there were no signs of life. It was all too neat and tidy. Where are the bikes that should be tossed carelessly in the front yard? The house was in mourning.

As time went on, we thought about the widow and her boys. I said little prayers for their wellbeing. For a simple prayer often holds the answer to life's complicated questions. I shared it with Terry. He agreed. But, it sounded silly to some of our friends and a little too generous to others. But, we thought differently. Sometimes it is best to act with our heart. And so I looked up the phone number of the young widow and gave her a call.

"Hello, my name is…" the conversation started out awkwardly and ended in joy.

For Gauge had not been born to be a hunting

dog, but a healing dog.

He was not quite two years old when he met his new family that lived a few miles from our front door. He would become the loving companion of two boys and their mother. His hunting days were behind him replaced with sports, school events and backyard games.

When we saw the reaction of the boys and their mother we realized it was a match made in heaven. The dog took off with the boys in their backyard as soon as he got out of the truck.

Gauge found his calling. He was meant to be loved by children. His slobbery kisses and cheerful heart were perfect for the kids. I often wondered how many adventures or misadventures they would all get in.

Naturally, we received plenty of phone calls asking us why our pretty white Gauge was seen at school events, football games and all over town with two boys. "I can't believe you gave that beautiful dog away. He must have cost a lot of money? What were you thinking?" one woman said. "Did they look happy?" I asked. "Yes, they were!" was her reply. That was all we needed to know.

Every now and then I would call to check on Gauge. We loved him after all. But, as long as things were working out and everyone was happy, that was all that mattered.

By now the boys are men. I do not know if their mother ever remarried. For that matter, we do not know if happy-go-lucky Gauge is still alive. But, we do know he put a smile on the faces of the two little boys who lost their father. His purpose was to bring joy. Sometimes we do not know our purpose until we are called to it. It seems Gauge was wiser than we gave him credit after all. He probably wondered what took us so long to figure it out.

THE FLY-AWAY HORSE

Oh, a wonderful horse is the Fly-Away Horse–
Perhaps you have seen him before;
Perhaps, while you slept, his shadow has swept
Through the moonlight that floats on the floor.
For it's only at night, when the stars twinkle bright,
That the Fly-Away Horse, with a neigh
And a pull at his rein and a toss of his mane,
Is up on his heels and away!
The moon in the sky,
As he gallopeth by,
Cries: "Oh! What a marvelous sight!"
And the Stars in dismay
Hide their faces away
In the lap of old Grandmother night.

—*Eugene Field*

CHAPTER FIVE

TRAVELER

*A*ndersen *windows*, pastel hued stained glass panels, ivory colored kitchen cupboards, doors, woodwork, Tiffany dining room chandelier, deep pile white carpet, mahogany stained wooden floors sounded beautiful. So did the quaint fireplace and tall ceilings throughout the cottage. We chose dark colored egg-shaped doorknobs to set off the white woodwork. We planned on a big front porch, and a master bedroom with a French door that led to a sweet little deck that led to our backyard. Yes, it was truly going to be a romantic home. The house was much like the first quaint home I built in a small town years and years ago. Only this home was not cedar. This one was a refined version of the first one. It was sophisticated. Rather than wood siding we opted for sage-colored *James Hardie*. I no longer was strong enough to stain a house every couple of years. It was tedious, messy work that should be done to preserve the natural beauty of wood siding. Those days were over. This home was to be our retirement home when that day arrived.

We planned everything down to the last nail. It had a small kitchen, but it was quite beautiful and filled with brand-new bright appliances. A stone fireplace added whimsy as well. We planted various trees, shrubs and flowers. We worked alongside our contractor and painted, stained, and worked hard on our dream home. I chose an intricate carving to put above the porch, a sort of whimsical decorative piece that had a fairy tale look. When we finally completed the home we stood back to admire it. One would think we would be thrilled, but something lingered in both of us that we could not explain. What was it? Surely it wasn't the new home? It was such a beautiful cottage. We planned for this day. What was missing? Why didn't the new house thrill us? It felt strangely hollow.

I knew in my soul what the problem was. But, I did not tell anyone, even my husband. I feared it would hurt him or make him feel I was not grateful for the new house we worked so hard on. It remained a secret from him for quite some time. It had nothing to do with our pretty dream house, but a beloved pet.

Nine months before the completion of our home, we sold our little acreage that sat forty miles north. It was near Palisades State Park, outside Garretson, SD. It was simply too far for my husband to commute to work five or six days a week with gas prices so high. Sometimes I worried about his safety in the winter months as well. It was not a straight route; it was a complicated one. Anything can happen to a commuter in the winter months and often does. So, we made the decision to move into the town where he was employed, sell our acreage and our horses. Besides, I was no longer the rider of my youth and arthritis took a toll. We both felt it was a wise choice. It was a very rational decision we told ourselves. It did not upset me to say goodbye to the dusty buckskin colt Timber. He had a perfect new owner, a young art teacher who trained horses. We were pleased to see Chip go to the Rapid City Stock Show because he was a mean-tempered bully. He found a job on a ranch West River. Perhaps an honest job would make him an honest horse we thought.

Now there was one problem that we both tried hard to ignore: Traveler.

"Horses, if God made anything more beautiful,
He kept them for Himself."
—Author Unknown

He reminded me of chaps and boots the first time I saw him. He simply shined! Images of a Western movie suddenly appeared out of nowhere. His effect was that powerful. I tried to reason with myself, but it was useless. I loved him the moment we met.

He was a mix of youth, strength and beauty. It can be a dangerous combination and I knew better. But, all reason was cast aside just to spend more time with the three-year-old Paint horse. Now, long ago I learned that looks are not everything in men or horses. Good looks can often disguise mean or selfish natures. However, all he had to do was look my way and I was doomed. He had a certain something, no doubt about it. There was no going back. His papered name was Traveling Man. The name fit him perfectly for he sure could travel, spin around and stand his ground. He was a proud one indeed. Traveling Man had been a stallion. However, his flashy pattern did not show up in his pretty offspring. He actually had a perfect "H" on his left side. It stood for handsome, more or less in my eyes, and I guess his too. His pretty foals were solid colored for some reason. Therefore, a decision was made to geld him. Even though he was gelded, his proud mannerisms remained intact. He was a tad defiant. Oh, the rebel in him was glorious. If only common sense ruled me that day instead of blind love.

The first time I rode him he was mannerly, although prone to putting his head up now and then. I remember saying a little prayer to St. Francis and blessing myself. He did not buck nor did he try to kick or bite. I took it as a good sign. He looked a little sad that he was expected to carry me nonetheless.

When I dismounted my arthritis betrayed me. My leg buckled in pain and gave way. Slowly, I fell close to his left front leg in an pile. It is not a good place to be. Instead of jumping back, kicking or stepping on me, he just looked down with what appeared to be pity. At that moment, I loved his intelligent understanding. For not a half hour prior to my getting into the saddle he dragged his trainer around the pen like a rag doll. He did not tolerate that trainer nor did he tolerate the next three... But, Traveling Man had a soft spot for me it seemed. The group standing around noticed it as well. It was a grand moment. The horse and I seemed to be the mutual admiration society.

A deal was struck that day. Traveler had a home with us.

The road was not always a smooth one with Traveler. He was kind to all manner of beasts and human beings as long as he was not ridden. Dogs, cats, other horses all found a gentle, beautiful pal with him. But, he had a bad habit, a dangerous one. He bolted! A rider knows a horse that bolts is dangerous. One minute he could be going along slowly, the next take off, and slam on the brakes. It was problematic with him. I enlisted the help of very knowledgeable trainers, gentle horse whisperer types or seasoned horse people. Trav had both women and men trainers. They all gave me the same sage advice: sell him. My head told me it was logical, but my heart could not bear to say goodbye.

I will never forget one early autumn day when Traveler pulled his famous bolting act. My husband and a friend witnessed it. He bolted and I went in another direction, landed on my left side and suffered a blunt force injury. I remember thinking broken bones hurt less. But, at the urging of my husband and friend I got up and walked bravely up the little hill. In a few months I had internal bleeding. It seems the injury was serious enough.

As the years passed I looked at Traveler with an understanding it was just his way. Many times people would question my love for him. But, I respected his unwillingness to be ridden. Why can't a person love an animal just for being themselves?

"As a good horse is not apt to jump over a bank, if left to guide himself, I let mine pick his own way." —Buffalo Bill

One night I had an unusual dream. In the dream Traveler was walking in flowers... When I told my husband early the next morning we both laughed. What a silly dream! However, when we went downstairs, opened the patio door there stood Traveling Man! He was waiting for us by the downstairs patio door.

We found where he had crawled under the fence to escape the relentless bullying of Chip, the buckskin. Traveler could simply take it no more and decided to get down on his knees, and lift part of the fence with his back and walk to the patio door… We found his hoof prints in the flower bed by the back door the next morning. Rather than go into the corn field, or on the highway, he simply waited for us to get up the next day. My husband never got over the dream, nor will I.

Yes, Traveler was a character. He allowed dogs to sleep with him in the pasture, cats to drink from his water tank, and greeted visitors at the fence and gate. He hated baths but loved to be brushed. I tried giving him sponge baths only to have him roll in the mud like a dog. However, he knew how to back up like a big Mack Truck to have his tail combed. He would stand for an hour or more to have his thick tail untangled, combed and brushed. He would put his forehead next to mine and sigh. He even liked having a saddle on for some reason. We never understood why he could tolerate the saddle, but not a rider. He looked proud when he had a saddle on, but as soon as we got in the saddle his disposition would change. Sometimes he would walk slowly and just stop. But, other times he would just take off—zoom! A rider would need to be mindful of his speed, agility and determination.

When the day came to part with Traveler, it was my turn to bolt. After six years he was my pet and pal.

I advertised Traveler and many people responded. I felt they were not good fits. Then one day a woman called. She sounded sweet. She saw his photo online and like me, fell in love. She had over 1000 acres, and not too far from our home. She also had a lovely home and a teenage daughter. They were in the cattle business. When they came out I liked them. My husband and I told them Traveler would take a confident rider. They assured us they were fully capable of handling him as well as treating him well. Traveler behaved like a gentleman. I was a little upset that he was so mannerly. Now, he would be sold for sure!

As if by cue to match my mood, it started to rain softly. It was a gray, wet day when Traveler was loaded into their big trailer. He started to whinny and then stomped. He knew, and I knew it was goodbye.

That evening I wept. Sleep did not come easily. My side ached and I was diagnosed with diverticulitis. What a mean ailment... stress? Through it all I kept trying to focus on the new house, work or family matters. But, it did not last long and my thoughts always drifted to Traveler.

A few days later we were outside, trimming bushes and mowing. Out of habit I looked at the pasture and couldn't see Traveler. Suddenly, I remembered and felt odd. The pasture was vacant and empty. I felt a lump in my throat and fought it back. It was no good. Tears rolled down my face and at that moment I knew I betrayed myself.

I ran to the phone and called the new owner.

When she answered I asked how Traveler was. "It has only been one week. Things are working out well," she replied. It comforted me a little bit.

The next week I called again. Again, she told me everything was working out well, for the most part.

What did she mean, for the most part?

"Why don't you come out this weekend and see for yourself. He is coming along nicely. It won't be long and I am sure my daughter and I will have a great trail horse," she said.

The next Saturday we took the little journey to see how Traveler was doing. When we drove up their long driveway we were impressed. There stood a gorgeous home, with a view of the James River. It was splendid. The woman and her daughter came out to see us while her husband worked with cattle.

She walked us over to where they kept Traveler. When he saw us he started to whiny loud and run around his fenced in area. He greeted us with nickers and nuzzling. I realized at that moment how much he meant to both of us.

The woman asked if we would like to come inside to have a cold beverage and freshen up. It was a warm and humid day. When we turned to walk away all of a sudden Traveler lifted the gate latch and ran all the way down the embankment towards the James River. Oh no! Somebody forgot to lock the latch! Without a fence and endless river bottom, trees and brush who knows where he could end up? It was serious. He did not know the area and obviously these people did not know him.

My husband calmly asked for a halter, turned and walked carefully down the steep embankment. It took him considerable time. At the bottom of the hill we saw Traveler running back and forth in a frenzy. He was not himself. He was in a panic.

Yet, when the horse realized it was Terry, his frantic behavior stopped, he walked up and put his beautiful head down like a dog. Terry slipped the halter on and they walked calmly the half mile together. The woman was quiet. She apologized for the mishap and vowed they would never let anything like that happen again. I wondered... I prayed she would not be so careless again.

Traveler thought he was going home with us. We betrayed him once again. His head picked up as he noticed us walk towards our car. His eyes were once again filled with fear and confusion. He bellowed and cried out in a shrill voice. Never before or since, have I heard a horse cry out in such a heart wrenching manner. Some people call it a scream, but it was worse. It was a deep sort of sound, it was horrible. He was crying out in despair. We came all this way just to see if he was alright. Clearly he was not, nor were we. Just because he had food and shelter did not make it right. I knew it, and so did my husband. But by that time we had the house plans, contractor and lot picked out. Things surely would work out with Traveler and his new family, they just had to.

Over the course of six months I called often. I never spent the money she gave me for Traveler for some reason. It remained in my little safe.

Nine months passed. I needed to do something but what? Oh, I knew the answer as odd as it seemed.

I picked up the phone and called the woman about Traveler one more time. I wanted him and was praying she would understand. I was determined to find a good place for him near us. But, first I had to convince the woman to sell him back to us. With hope in my heart and fingers crossed, I dialed her number and waited…

She had an icy tone when she heard my voice. "We moved Traveler in with the bulls! My husband does not like him. So, he put him in with the bulls."

I nearly fainted. Yet, I did not want to alienate her and had to remain calm…

"I would really love to buy Traveler back. We miss him. I hope you understand," I said quietly.

"That is fine with me. We were getting ready to advertise him. It seems you and the Paint horse are an item. He bucked our daughter off and broke her arm! He also injured my tailbone. We no longer like him. You can buy him back for what I paid. It is best you come get him!"

I was overjoyed. "Oh, by the way, you might as well keep the saddle, I won't be needing it anymore. We will be just fine without it," I replied.

By the next weekend I found a place two miles

from our new house. I went from acreage to acreage and farm to farm within a five-mile radius. Some people were kind, others not so much. At the last door a very lovely lady answered. When she saw my look of distress, she thought I had been in an accident. I guess my desperation was pretty obvious. She was a fairy godmother if ever there was one. Her home and farm were absolutely beautiful, just like her. As it turns out she was a widow. Her large barn no longer held cattle, sheep or horses. Traveler would have his own little shed, and his own little pasture. He would be less than two miles from our front door. It was a good start.

We made arrangements to have someone pick Traveler up and drop him off to his new surroundings. I called our fine horse vet to check on his condition. He was in pretty good shape except for a large bite on his rump. We never did know what happened to him when he was in the bull pen. He had lost considerable weight too. We found that his feet needing trimming and he had not been given his shots or wormed. We never understood why.

"Well, it is a perfect match—one made in heaven. The woman who can't ride anymore and the horse nobody could ever ride," the sage vet said. I teared up when he said it. He always reminded me of Will Rogers in wisdom and charm. Yes, I no longer can ride or walk anymore without a great deal of pain. It all makes perfect sense that I bought Traveler back.

In June we put our brand new house on the

market. It sold in a matter of days. We never had an open house. I was getting my hair cut one day and told the stylist our house was on the market. "Oh, my mother and father in-law from Tennessee are looking at country places today. They want to make a decision soon. They loved living in the country and have been searching for a cute place nearby," she said cheerfully.

"Oh, that's too bad, our house is in town. But it is very pretty with a big front porch," I remember saying.

However, within minutes after getting home from the salon, a car pulled up and a man got out and rang our doorbell. It was a real estate agent. Within two hours the house was sold for the asking price. The couple must have been enchanted! It thrilled us because they were the first and only people who walked through the door. After all, the sign was just put in the front yard!

We rented a town house until we could find a place in the country. We went full circle. There was a lesson in this. I just knew it. Never second guess your heart.

It was the month of October when we moved into an older home with five acres. It needed new siding, a new furnace, and new air conditioning. But, it had five pretty acres though, three in rich green grass. A little shed sat on the pasture too for extra hay storage. The interior of the house exuded warmth and charm. It was precious and drew me in. It had a vintage feel with coved ceilings and old fashioned linen colored kitchen cupboards. It was truly quaint. For the outside of the house did not do justice to the inside. It was a sweet little abode reminiscent of a simpler time. The moment I walked through door I felt the house welcome us. Indeed, there was something familiar about it. Eerily we found out the house had been moved on the property thirty years ago from my childhood neighborhood in Sioux Falls. No wonder it felt like a hug.

We immediately went to work on fencing, and put up a new shed for Traveler that faces our bedroom. He would love the privacy and we would love seeing him just outside our windows. The pasture bordered seventy acres of CRP on the south and farmland to the north and east filled with wildlife. He would no longer have to contend with angry bulls.

If I have my way, we will grow old together. I love him so… he was always a smart fellow. After all, he has me pretty well trained. Not a day goes by I don't greet him first thing in the morning and the last thing at night. His life is filled with apples, carrots, and affection. A horse is God's noblest creature in my eyes… I share my secrets with him and he listens. If I walk slowly he does too. When I need to lean on him for support he stands quietly. His patience is amazing. I often wonder just how much he understands… No, he never became a performance horse or a halter horse as many thought he was bred for. Instead, his purpose was to be loved for what he was, not what others felt he should be. There is much to be said about allowing all living creatures to simply be.

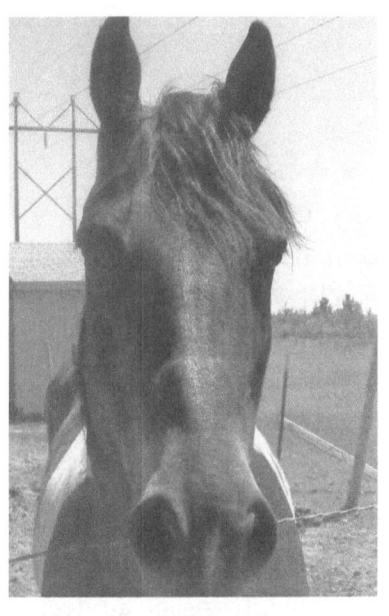

CHAPTER SIX

BUTTERMILK

"What is your favorite color?"
How many times are we asked this question throughout our life? It is basic.

What shade do you prefer? Ask any salesperson. Whether it is clothing, a vehicle, interior or exterior paint, hair color, eye color, the list is probably endless. How many times do we choose something based purely on the superficial? I am ashamed to admit I have. "Don't judge a book by its cover" is not simply a worn cliché. It is sage advice.

Years ago children and adults enjoyed TV westerns. *Hopalong Cassidy, Roy Rogers* and *The Lone Ranger* were a few of the cultural icons of the 1950s. These characters set good examples. Years later *Bonanza* became a favorite which is easy to understand. Between the adorable Little Joe, kind hearted Hoss, noble, wise father figure in Ben, and brooding older brother Adam, the show was hard to resist. I remember how sad my aunts felt when Adam left the show. I think they had crushes on Pernell Roberts. The only crush I had was on Little Joe, Michael Landon. Nevertheless, his spectacular paint horse(s) took center stage in my eyes. Westerns could be a little goofy no doubt. Still, others had more adult themes such as *Gunsmoke, Rawhide, Wanted Dead or Alive,* or even *The Rifleman.* Of course, compared to today's viewing these are tame. Nevertheless, they all held lessons on right and wrong. The plots were often basic and unsophisticated. However, these TV time machines all have one thing in common: the symbolism of the steed.

As a little girl I was immediately drawn to the pretty horses. The "bad guys" never rode the pretty horses. Instead, they seemed to ride nondescript ones. Of course, TV was mostly black and white so the viewer would not be able to differentiate between a blue roan, black, sorrel or bay. However, they could spot a pristine white, golden palomino, flashy paint or gorgeous buttermilk buckskin.

Dale Evans had it made in my opinion. She may not have ridden the spectacular Trigger, but he was Roy's horse after all. Her horse was a sweet faced buttermilk buckskin. Even the name Buttermilk made me feel secure and cozy. Images of red checkered table cloths, neatly stacked golden pancakes, warm maple syrup, generous dollops of butter and delicious, crisp bacon all came to mind.

Yes, some words or names evoke goodness.

Whenever the stunning palomino and lovely buckskin pranced in front of our little TV screen my child's heart beat faster. I felt the black tipped ears and matching black socks contrasted beautifully with the creamy coat of Dale's beloved Buttermilk. The little buckskin was a beauty for sure. Yes, Dale Evans had it made no doubt. She had Buttermilk and the pretty shepherd dog Bullet. Although I never felt Bullet was any match for Rin Tin Tin. But, that is another story... Yes, Dale Evans, could not possibly want or need any more than her wonderful, faithful horse.

One day I thought to myself, I will have my own Buttermilk.

Thirty-five years passed.

"Hey, what do you think of this one? He's special. Just look at that color!" I said.

"How much?" my husband asked.

"Well, a little more than I want to spend," I replied.

"Better think twice," he said seriously.

The photo tempted me. So, I shut off the computer, went outside and did a few chores. I needed to clear my head.

That night I could not get the buttermilk out of my head. I tossed and turned. Finally, I got up, went downstairs and turned on the computer once again. His image drew me in, tempted me like Pandora's Box. I set the wheel in motion...

So we drove to Cannon Falls, Minnesota to see a horse named Chip. He had a far more regale registered name, but Chip was what he was known by. What a beautiful place I thought to myself when driving through the town. We found the ranch where the gelding lived equally lovely. The sellers were kind, friendly, helpful and knowledgeable. To this day we are friends.

Chip didn't disappoint. He was for all practical purposes, a looker. He was well behaved although a tad spirited. I rode him out alone in their large pasture. It had little hilly areas which he navigated beautifully. I admired his manners. Yet, I had a little trepidation because I did not have a helmet on. Sure, they do not look cool, but they are lifesavers. I didn't really know this horse. We were strangers. What if he bolted, bucked, or reared? What was I thinking? In my excitement I neglected the most important rule, safety. For a moment I had second thoughts about the horse but pushed them away. Looking back, was it a premonition?

Luckily nothing unpleasant occurred while I rode the horse. It was a smooth ride and things looked like they would work out for everyone, including my pal Traveler. He had been alone and now he would have a pasture pal at long last.

Two weeks later a horse trailer pulled up with Chip. Our friends unloaded him. We walked him through the yard, opened the gate and let him get used to his new surroundings. We also divided the

pasture in such a way that both Traveler and Chip would not end up squabbling. In time we would allow the horses to come together as friends, or so we hoped. For the time being they could introduce themselves in a safe manner. There was no need to rush.

That night we watched both horses stand next to one another quietly with only the fence between them. It looked promising. The sight of them thrilled me. My childhood dreams were finally realized. Dale Evans would have approved.

It was a short lived hope.

Over the course of a month, we found Chip had a jealous grudge against Traveler. He had it in for him one could easily see. If Traveler trotted over to visit us Chip would pin his ears back and make a bee-line for Traveler. He didn't stop there. He was not happy until he bit Traveler. These were not little nips. No, the bites were often vicious. Now, Traveler was not prepared for his new pasture pal to be so mean-spirited. He looked hurt and stunned. I guess we all were. This was not acceptable.

So, we went to great lengths to keep the horses apart. Half the pasture would be Chip's, the other half Traveler's. The little barn had two Dutch door entries. Therefore, each horse had a separate entry if they were going to be stalled. Yet, Chip would always push the limits. Sometimes he would reach as far as he could over the fence hoping to bite Traveler. Worse yet, he would try to push the fence down completely to get into Traveler's area to wage an attack.

After a few months, it appeared Chip was mellowing out. Perhaps the worst was over. We opened the gate that divided the two pastures and the horses at last were together. It was autumn so the horses depended more on hay instead of pasture grass. We always divided the hay into 4-5 separate feeding areas. That way Chip would be focused on his meal and not Traveler. Our scheme never worked. It failed miserably. Rather than focus on eating, Chip took it upon himself to drive Traveler away from every single little hay mound. Back and forth he ran, teeth barred, ears pinned looking like a demon instead of a sweet faced creamy-coated dream gelding. He was unrelenting in his brutality. Finally, we decided to always put Traveler inside a stall, feed him and keep Chip outside in the pasture.

The old saying "Be careful what you wish for" finally made sense.

This pattern became a routine. We always had to be on our toes with Chip. Granted, he was well mannered with me the whole time. I started to deeply resent his cruelty to Trav. Somehow Traveler never retaliated. He fled instead. The little Paint could usually outmaneuver the larger horse. We never once saw him bite Chip. But, Traveler had finally had enough.

One day the bully otherwise known as Chip had Traveler in a corner. We ran out to save Traveler when all of a sudden he turned around and kicked Chip square in his chest! THUMP! Chip looked stunned and backed up slowly. Traveler left his mark. Two horseshoe marks were tattooed on the buckskin's chest. After the vet said Chip would be alright we were relieved. He respected Traveler after that. Perhaps the buckskin would "live and let live" and life would be peaceful.

Well, as the weeks passed things were tranquil. We never saw Chip attack Traveler again. In fact, they kept a distance from one another. Yet, it was not the end of Chip's bullying.

One day my husband decided to ride Chip around the pasture. All this time a storm was brewing in the buckskin. His next move could have proved fatal.

As Chip trotted by he glanced back at Traveler, took off with my husband at a full gallop and bucked high in the air… My husband was thrown about 20 feet, landed hard and was disorientated. It looked like a PRCA rodeo instead of our pasture. I felt faint but immediately dialed 911, gave directions, hung up the phone and ran into the pasture to his side. He acted like it was nothing, but I knew better. Soon friends from the fire department and EMS arrived. He was lucky to be alive given the distance he flew. He suffered no broken bones or internal injuries. But, he did have a slight concussion. I will never forget that day. It could have been far worse, but it shouldn't have happened at all.

I had one of his friends take Chip's saddle off and lead him in the stall. The horse looked smug. What a miserable creature for all his flash. But, I had my own plan for the bully. He was going to get an honest job far, far away and it couldn't come soon enough. No more reprieves for Chip. His days were numbered around our place. How I detested him.

Now I knew why he was given the name Chip. He had a huge chip on his shoulder. He was no more than sour buttermilk plain and simple.

I made arrangements to have Chip taken to the Rapid City Stock Show. A working cattle ranch out west bought him where he would work hard for his keep the rest of his life. I doubt he remained king of the hill. He was a looker alright and fetched a fair sum. Harmony was restored. Traveler was soon prancing and dancing and we finally got a good night's rest.

Not before or since, have I detested a living creature like that drop-dead gorgeous horse. The only good that came of having him was learning a hard, humiliating lesson. Bullies are not just people. They can be animals too. They can hide their nastiness with a stunning mask of beauty. But, their beauty soon corrodes when their true ugliness is exposed. The world should not tolerate bullies no matter how clever or beautiful.

Now, when somebody asks me what my favorite color of horse is I reply, "Safe, yes safe is the prettiest color."

"I Ride An Old Paint"

I ride an old paint, I lead an old dan
I'm goin' to Montana to throw the hoolihan
They feed in the coulees, they water in the draw
Their tails are all matted, their backs are all raw

Ride around little dogies, ride around them slow
For the fiery and snuffy are rarin' to go

When I die, take my saddle from the wall
Place it on my old pony, lead him out of his stall
Tie my bones to my saddle and turn our faces to the West
And we'll ride the prairie we love the best

Ride around little dogies, ride around them slow
For the fiery and snuffy are rarin' to go

I ride an old paint, I lead an old dan
I'm goin' to Montana to throw the hoolihan
They feed in the coulees, they water in the draw
Their tails are all matted, and their backs are all raw

Ride around little dogies, ride around them slow
For the fiery and snuffy are rarin' to go

~ 71 ~

"*We need the tonic of wildness… At the same time that we are earnest to explore and learn new things, we require that all things be mysterious and unexplorable, that land and sea be indefinitely wild, unsurveyed and unfathomed by us because unfathomable. We can never have enough of nature.*"

—Henry David Thoreau
Walden: Or, Life in the Woods

CHAPTER SEVEN

DAN

*"The happiest man is he who learns
from nature the lesson of worship.*
—Ralph Waldo Emerson

Subconsciously, I drift in and out. I learned long ago to sleep with one eye open. My skin feels clammy, cool and wet to the touch. My head pounds with a dull ache. My blankets were tossed sometime in the night leaving my skin exposed to the night air or worse. I was in battle again, the same nightmare… It has been years since I felt the sweet bliss of a good night's rest. In the distance a monotone voice delivers a weather report. Why can't it be a tune instead? For a few seconds I forget my name. Terror fills me. I struggle to collect myself taking slow, deep breaths. This has happened many times since I got back. I am familiar with the drill. At last, my temporary amnesia slowly disappears.

I live with a lot of ghosts. They are my constant companions. Their blurred images cross my days and nights. What do they want? It has taken a heavy toll. Often I forget who I am and why I am still here.

Slowly I stretch. It feels good. I check myself and am relieved that everything is still intact. I look and feel much older than I am. I shake the nightmares off and ready myself. Nightmares are routine and I grapple with them. Silently, I remember my gear placed the night before. It is time to step quietly into the shadows. My mission has begun.

I have the checklist embedded in my mind. Do I come in from the west or from the southwest? Have they bedded all night? I must be silent. Much depends on the wind direction and temperature. I must not let them know my position.

I go through the things I need to carry—poncho, ammo pouch, canteen, bayonet, shovel, ammo, M-16, grenades, machete, around eighty pounds I think... No wonder they call us Grunts.

Wait, no, this can't be right. I am still groggy. Start over. I need my bow, skinning-knife, extra pair of socks, water bottle and a couple of granola bars. Yes, that is more like it.

Opening the door, I notice heavy frost has covered everything in its path. It is striking. I am overtaken with it and tears start to well up. It is strange. I wonder why? I keep my emotions hidden. Thankfully, nobody is here to witness the tears. I brush them from my face. I allow myself to breathe in the stark, clean splendor surrounding me. It clears my head. I am grateful to escape, if only for a moment, the prison I built around me.

At last I reach my destination.

My hunting supplies are light compared to the drab olive green of war. My hands and shoulders have carried many burdens, but none as heavy as what lies in my soul.

Checking the wind constantly, I slowly, methodically, try to work my way to the tree stand which is quite a distance. How far? I count each step, an old habit from childhood. Isn't life measured in the steps we take? One step out of line and we are reminded of our transgressions.

The air is crisp and my senses are on high alert. I trudge on, stopping and pausing to feel if the wind has picked up. Did it switch directions? No, that is good. I listen for movement ahead of me or off to the sides just like in Vietnam. I stop, crouch, look. I strain my eyes to see in the pre-dawn darkness. What do I expect to see, more ghosts? But, the only sounds come from my labored breathing and drumming of my heart. Tiny ice crystals form on my mustache with each breath. The pre-dawn chill is exhilarating. It pleases me. I have a strong heart like my grandfather, Jens. He was a full blooded Dane who immigrated to America, a true Viking by anyone's standards. Like him, my heart has weathered many hardships. I continue. The jungle may be far from South Dakota, but it lives in my darkest memories. I pick up the clean masculine scent of weathered wood, perhaps cedar? It helps drive the dank humid jungle from my head and all its suffering.

It's early November. Christmas is not far away. Christmas was my favorite holiday as a little boy. I loved it. It was the magical time filled with innocence, joy, peace and hope.

My innocence is long gone. I wonder, is there a reason to believe in hope?

In the early morning hour, a horned owl swoops down so close to my face that I feel the wind from his silent wings, exhilarating and horrifying. Impressive bird so stealthy, was he warning me of something or reminding me just who is the prey?

Cautious on my feet, trying not to crunch the dry twigs, sneaking, stop, sneaking stop, sneaking, stop. It is a ritual to be ever mindful of where my feet fall... Never make a sound!

As I am slowly working closer, I can hear the trickle of the creek before me, about seventy-five yards ahead. I ponder. Should I wash my hands in the semi-frozen water, a sort of baptism?

I methodically feel my way through the pre-dawn darkness—glad I memorized the way. As I come to the creek, I remember one must drop down the steep bank in order to cross it. My hands and feet find the old path known only by those that crossed long before me. It is an ancient trail.

The water is shallow, maybe six inches rippling over the rocks. Good, it is not yet frozen. It is completely hidden by an unruly overgrowth, a haven for wild things. Only the determined would attempt to follow such a rugged path. I love this secret place and what it holds.

I wash my hands in the coldness of the stream and it thrills my senses. I am alert. Crossing and going up the bank, I hear the rustling of the ancient cottonwood trees. My ears pick up an unfamiliar sound in the distance. It must be the wind. Or has something picked up my scent after all? It may just be a rabbit or coyote moving through. I can't say because it is still somewhat dark.

I wait for a minute though it seems much longer. I want to make sure that whatever moved has settled down—no use taking a chance. Just ahead of me lies a steep grade hill. I must climb it to reach my destination.

One wrong step on burr oak acorns and their crunch will give me away. The path is littered with them. I must remember to gather some before I leave. I must continue…

Am I slow enough, methodical enough? Precision and timing, precision and timing, precision and timing, the endless chant plays in my head. It's another 200 yards to go. Again, my mind goes over my equipment. Have the weeks and hours of practice been enough? Will they pay off this morning? Why do I doubt myself so much? Finally, at the top of the hill, I can just make out the tree.

Bordering a cornfield and the heavily wooded area, it towers before me. It is impressive. It is about fifty feet tall by eight feet in diameter, just a short distance from the river. It is a wise tree and I wonder what stories and secrets it holds? This is a favorite spot for deer because it is close to a massive cornfield and the Big Sioux.

I take a moment to listen for deer before I ascend. So far, I go undetected. I place my bow on a low branch and ease my way into the tree. Reaching down, I lift my bow and place it on my shoulder. My fingers cling to the heavy bark as I ascend higher and higher, hugging it tightly with my arms and legs. It is an intimate feeling, one with nature. It comforts me. My younger days of tree climbing truly paid off. My mother used to call me her little monkey. She worried I would fall, but I never did. I recollect my childhood treehouse. It was a refuge of sorts from all of life's disappointments and fears. It held my dreams as well as victories. It listened like a good friend. Perhaps that is why I choose to sit within the branches unlike many hunters. It can be trusted.

I melt into the tree and we become one.

I feel a tree stand would only give my favorite location away to other hunters. I am possessive of the venerable tree. Suddenly, a bushy tailed squirrel scampers the trunk and takes refuge on my arm. I am pleased the tree has hidden me so well. Realizing my arm is not a branch and only inches from my face, it is startled. Bushy tail quickly flees, chattering all the way down the trunk. I smile thinking how foolish it felt. I check my Bear Alaskan Compound Bow one last time for arrows to be secured. I knock an arrow and ready myself.

Birds are starting to chirp. How brave they are to weather the harsh Dakota winter. I hear mice, rabbits and squirrels rummaging in the dry, frosty leaves for food. It has not snowed yet.

Just then, I notice a reddish light slowly rising to the east—sunrise. It startles me with its beauty.

I have already been up for three hours. Should I have stayed in my warm bed? No, it is good being out here. I am quite comfortable with my back to the tree some fifteen feet in the air. The tree seems to caress me in its giant arms. It holds my weight with ease and I am almost lulled to sleep...

What is this? It is a lazy latecomer lumbering along hoping to find a deer stand of his own. He has no idea he is invading my territory. I enjoy the shock in his stupid eyes as he notices mine glare, flashing a warning to back down. He is embarrassed, nods, and quickly goes back in the direction he came from. Good riddance. That is what happens when one is unprepared or haphazard. They find themselves in places they do not belong. They miss much. They never learned to read signs. I am here to stay and it pleases me the lazy hunter did not detect me nestled in the branches.

In the distance I hear crunching. It seems to stop and start.

Slowly, I turn my head to the sound. I can just make it out. I catch enough light to see a doe and yearling some fifty yards away. They start grazing in my direction, ears and nose in alert. She has nothing to fear from me. I am not after them. Just then she pauses thirty yards away and gently turns her head searching for possible danger. However, she can't see me, nor smell me. The wind is in my favor. She continues to stare at something which is headed in our direction. She walks closer and stops.

Could this be the prize buck I have been patiently waiting for? I wait.

Just then, I realize what the doe was gazing at, a buck headed this way. The pretty doe and yearling flee. Oh no, they picked up my scent after all! I see the silhouette of the buck. He must not have detected me. How can that be? Surely if the doe knew of my presence wouldn't the buck? From my vantage point he appears to be around three, maybe four years old. As he gracefully steps forward, my eyes are momentarily blinded by the brilliant kaleidoscope colors of sunrise. Shielding them, I notice his coat shimmers. It is totally white! It must be an illusion. I need to steady myself. I have heard of such deer but never thought I would witness one. My mind is racing with excitement. He is pure white without blemish. White-on-white, the area surrounding me glitters with brilliant sunbeams. The tender young buck almost sparkles. I am taken aback, rub my eyes and stare in wonderment. Is this a dream? I adjust my eyes again amazed.

The ethereal deer stands directly underneath my stand. I am spellbound. I know albino deer are rare.

His antlers appear to be white porcelain. He lifts his beautiful head and looks up to me tucked high in the branches. I almost hear the white buck speak "I saw you before you saw me." I feel foolish and ashamed. The deer senses my guile. Yet, he does not show fear. Nor does he make a sound. Instead, he is quiet and paws the ground gently. His tail seems to flicker a little, but for the most part, all is silent and unmoving.

I notice his long white lashes frame crystal blue eyes. Albinos have pink eyes. I am confused. In turn he searches my green eyes. His unwavering glance seems to last a long time. It unsettles me. What is happening? I do not move as he studies me. Silver wisps of breath escape from his fine nostrils into the frosty air. Everything is still. Why doesn't he bolt? Still, he shows no fear. What is happening? This is wonderful and bizarre. I want to reach down and touch his beautiful coat. For a few seconds I wish to follow the white deer. He holds me spellbound. He seems opaque. His strange beauty transcends time and place.

I am overwhelmed with humility and have no desire to take his splendid life.

Like a mirage he fades into the undergrowth and forest. His steps are faint and then no more. All is silent. Did I dream this?

"God passes through the thicket of the world,
And wherever His glance falls, He turns all things to
beauty." — St. John of the Cross

I gather my thoughts… I conjure up the ghost of my best buddy and childhood friend, Dan. His memory is never far away. I can't seem to bury the past. He was movie-star handsome, good natured and fun-loving. We were just eighteen and straight out of high school when I was drafted. Selfishly I talked him into enlisting instead of attending college. After all, we always went through "thick and thin" together. School, career, and marriage could wait. We had all the bravado of young men. We were invincible.

But the first day of Boot Camp taught us to leave the bravado behind with the snarling, cryptic words of the Drill Sargent.

"Who in this line hunts? Take one step forward. Who in this line hunts big game? Take two more steps. Who in this line never hunted? Remain where you stand. Those of you who hunt big game stand a good chance. Those of who hunt occasionally have a slight chance. Those of you who have never carried a rifle or hunted, pray or learn to shoot."

Dan never hunted. He loved sports, especially football, and his pretty girlfriend, Cathy. He was a gentle good-natured person with a healthy conscience. He drove an old Chevy pickup, worked at a lumber yard and planned on attending college in the fall. He wasn't sure what direction his life would take, but he had his dreams. I miss his cheerful voice and corny jokes. He was beloved by all that knew him. Dan was a peacemaker. So when it was time to kill he hesitated and was killed instead. After all these decades I still can't get the image out of my head.

It haunts and tortures me. My best friend Dan was pure, a grown-up Boy Scout who loved, home, family and country. We were inseparable. Where I went, so did he. It was not fair that I came home without him. In a sense I never came back either... surviving is not the same as living.

Dan's destiny was to die at a tender age, never to grow old like me. Why couldn't I save him? When he stepped out into the predawn light the enemy shot him down. His intelligent blue eyes closed while his life poured out on a jungle floor thousands of miles from home. He had no chance. Why did I talk him into going to war with me?

Perhaps it was Dan's memory that stops me now from raising the bow and pulling the string. He was only eighteen, another promising young buck. Is that why I let the mystical blue-eyed albino deer live another season? I have no answer. Does it matter? All I feel is a lightness of being and a reason to hope. For I know now, Dan never blamed me for his coming home in a wooden box. I blamed myself.

Walking back to my truck, a long-forgotten childhood Christmas carol escapes my lips.

Epilogue

It's been over thirty years since I wrote about the albino deer in my journal. The only people that I finally shared the story with were close family members. It was not easy sharing the event that took place for many reasons. Now, some of them are gone and my story along with them.

Although I visit the area each year, I never use the venerable tree to hunt. Like me, it too is showing its age. We are growing old together, the tree and me. These days I prefer sitting under its mighty boughs. Its beauty is timeless and will remain my sanctuary of hope.

Strangely, it still appears to be hidden from the fast paced world. For that I am grateful. Sometimes my grandson and I search that special place hoping to see another albino deer, perhaps offspring of that magical buck. But we have never glimpsed one. The local farmers mention a myth-like deer that had been spotted by their grandparents long, long ago. I prefer to think of it though as Dan's deer.

CHAPTER EIGHT

❖

HANDSOME JACK
(BETTER WIT THAN WEALTH)

If ever a dog mirrored its owner, it was handsome Jack. His master was a mix of refinement and education, drinking and abandonment. Jack's master was a cheerful, blue-eyed free spirit one minute, a malcontent the next. His cynical wit caught many off guard. He was either loved or despised, depending on the remarks directed at the unsuspecting. With needle-like precision his words would find their target. His words held the truth and most people do not wish to be reminded of it. Therefore, he made both enemies and friends easily. People thought him either captivating or completely arrogant. There was no middle ground. He wore his auburn hair long, quoted writers and philosophers and spent time playing both flute and cello. He loved and respected God and nature, yet did not trust human beings, which was wise given mankind's proclivity for cruelty. Yes, Jack's master was scarred beyond repair like so many that travel life's bumpy roads. He saw too many deplorable things and met too many insincere people. One would never meet a more skeptical soul than Jack's master who had been wounded in love and life like so many of us. Yet, underneath the hard veneer was hidden a soft heart and a hard worker. He always gave freely to those he cared for deeply, none more than his beloved dog.

Handsome Jack was a splendid canine. He was ¾ German shepherd and ¼ Texas red wolf. He was born in Hill City, South Dakota. He was a big puppy with an inquisitive nature. His innate intelligence was apparent from his first months. Yet, like his owner, he pretty much did as he pleased which did not go over well with the lady of the house. The great American writer Washington Irving asked a clever question, "What tool gets sharper with use?" The answer is a woman's tongue. And, the lady of this house was no exception. The more the man and his dog did as they pleased, the sharper her words became. For Handsome Jack and his master were often the subjects of her anger and frustration. Certainly she loved both Jack and his master, she simply failed to understand them. For as charming as both the dog and his master were, they were not meant to be tied down. The two beautiful messes were always up to something. Frankly, they could be incorrigible.

Now science has shown that dog owners and their beloved pets resemble one another. This comparison extends beyond the physical. It extends to personality traits too. Perhaps it is all subconscious? Nevertheless, it seems more often than not that a dog is an extension of their owner. What do we wish to project? What does our heart follow? I have met people who choose a dog solely on their beauty. These dogs are stunning examples of fine breeding. Never mind if they are intelligent. On the other hand, some owners choose dogs for sport. They become trusted hunting companions or buddies. Then we have the breeds that are simply perfect companions for children. They are the perfect nanny. Sadly, some dogs are chosen to intimidate. For whatever reason their owners use them to impress upon others to "Watch out! We are to be reckoned with."

Yes, dogs convey their owners message to the outside world, a little like the vehicles they drive. Are they style statements for some people? Of course they are. It is wonderful to watch the dog shows just to see their owners. Do you wish to convey taste and refinement, strength and protectiveness, intelligence and dependability, agility and competitiveness, or beauty for beauty's sake? The dog show competitions are a stage for them all. It is a study in both human nature and dog behavior. I believe the happiest dog is the one who is chosen for friendship alone. They are loved for simply being no more than a best friend.

Jack was the latter. He was a buddy and followed his master everywhere, even a tavern or hideaway.

The woman of the house would often find herself wondering or worrying about their whereabouts. Like Rip Van Winkle, the man and dog would be long gone by the time she discovered them missing. And like Rip Van Winkle's Wolf, Jack was never happier than being by his master's side. His true wolf nature would take hold. One minute he would be napping by the fireplace, the next he would disappear only to be found the next morning seemingly hungover like his master. For when the mood would strike, the master would head out, big Jack on his heels. They were two of a kind.

The local bar owners would never turn away Handsome Jack. He seemed to draw business. He was cordial, and well mannered. Sometimes he had his own spot by the front door of the establishments. Of course, these days it is against regulations unless dog is a service dog. However, this was long ago.

Often the beautiful dog would patiently sit by his master's side at a table or stool for hours. Like his owner, he enjoyed the attention of the ladies. He was a beauty and knew it. His wild ways were hard to resist. The cunning of the dog matched the wit of his master.

Over time, the woman of the house grew increasingly impatient. It was only natural. The couple met quite young and fell in love. He felt she was beautiful and she felt he was fascinating. No doubt, they acted impetuously. Yet, they helped one another through school and life. They were great friends first, husband and wife afterwards.

One January evening a blizzard struck. The temperature was well below zero. It was a typical South Dakota blizzard, something to take seriously. It was time to hunker down. So, in a strange way it pleased her knowing the man would not visit his local haunts. She would have him to herself. Sometimes she would be lonely as they were a childless couple. She longed for his company and was planning on a cozy evening together watching TV or visiting. Furthermore, since they lived in the country, the roads would be impossible to navigate. No, this evening he would have to remain at home with her for a change.

She hummed to herself over the stove that evening. They would have a pot roast with all the trimmings—perfect for winter weather. Albeit she had a temper from time to time, she was a fine cook and housekeeper. She loved the man and his beautiful dog greatly. She was content they would weather the storm together. She glanced at the man reading a paper with Jack by his side. It gladdened her heart to know they were with her.

The aroma in the warm kitchen was enticing. The scents of beef roast, potatoes, carrots and onions blended with a homemade Dutch apple pie she made earlier in the day. As she set the table, she reminded him that supper was just about ready. Pulling aside the drape she glanced at the ever worsening storm. "Listen to the wind howling? It is getting worse. Look at the snow! It's really beautiful in its own way. The snowflakes are huge! I wonder how long it will last? Turn on the TV. Maybe they have a report?" she cheerfully said to him.

Turning around she noticed he was not there. "Dinner is ready!" she said, thinking he was in the bathroom. There was no answer. All of a sudden, she noticed Handsome Jack missing too. They vanished!

She quickly turned off the stove, put her parka and boots on, opened the door and saw in the distance the silhouette of her husband and Handsome Jack walking across the field. The brutal wind and sleet slashed her face fiercely. She quickly pulled her hair back to better see their ghost-like apparitions completely disappear. She called out to them once again, but only the wind replied. They were being called elsewhere and did not turn back. She knew she was defeated.

The following day they returned sharing the same sheepish demeanor. One could see they were guilty, but it was too late. The damage had been done. She was quiet, for the fight was gone from her. Instead, she was grateful no harm came to either one of them. At that moment she realized no words of chastisement, fine meal, or loving could change the man or his faithful wolf dog. In the end, she simply gave up trying to change them and thought to herself, "A leopard can't change its spots." Most people, as well as their pets, simply can't help their nature.

Whether we know it or not, our beloved dogs mimic us. When we shake hands, they lift a paw. When we are kind to others, they witness it. When we are intense or angry, they sense it. They are sponges, more or less. For one reason or another they mirror us.

Handsome Jack lived a good life, for the most part. He was a highly intelligent, graceful fellow. He made friends easily and knew how to disappear when trouble brewed. When he jumped a fence he looked like a gazelle, so full of grace and beauty. He was a unique fellow. Perhaps like his owner he was a little too clever at times. For they both often found themselves in precarious, almost dangerous situations from time to time. But, one still has to admire the free spirit in both animals and mankind. For nature in the end seems to have the upper hand. It is best to accept a dog or a person for what they are, not what we wish them to be.

CHAPTER NINE

BACKYARD TALES I: THE OWL

Ojibwa
Au
The owl
Au
The great black
Owl
Au
Hi! a! haa!
— Henry Wadsworth Longfellow

It was a clear October night when I finally pulled into our driveway. I taught evening classes and they ran late. So, I was anxious to grab a light snack, shower and climb into bed. But, this particular night I was in for a treat.

The headlights picked up something large and gray casually sitting on our front porch. What is this apparition I thought? At first I thought it was a coyote. However, my eyes deceived me. Instead of a bushy gray/beige fur coat it was a mass of fluffy gray/beige feathers dining on our front porch. It was a large horned owl!

Rather than fly away, he casually stared at me with calm dignity as if to say, "Do you care to join me? This is such a delicious rabbit."

I turned the headlights off and watched by the light of the moon. I was enthralled, yet somewhat shaken. It was like watching in slow motion. He took his time, relishing his meal. It was obvious he felt right at home. In a while, his powerful talons gripped what was left of the unfortunate little bunny and silently took flight, just passing over my windshield.

The next morning and many more, we found remnants of meals. Frankly, it was becoming unsettling. We would get up in the night to spy on his arrivals and departures. Yet, we seldom saw him. Nevertheless, the porch was not meant to be a diner. It was meant to welcome visitors with flowers.

Often we would see the mysterious bird float by just after sunset, perch on the utility pole crossarms and take command of his domain. He reminded me of a flying battleship. No doubt, the night sky was his vast ocean and he ruled supreme.

Last year he did not appear. We wondered if he had found another home or perhaps died. We both missed the bewitching bird of prey despite his poor table manners. He was a fascinating fellow.

One morning this July my husband stepped outside our front porch to take his first little stroll as part of his cancer recovery. The sun was lifting its golden head above a pink-tinted horizon, dew was glistening and all was still. The day held hope and promise.

With his first step he heard a soft "Hoo, hoo, how are you?" Then again, he heard "Hoo, hoo, how are you?"

Looking up he saw a large gray/beige horned owl perched comfortably in the tree. The big copper eyed bird looked directly at my husband and once again asked "Hoo hoo, how are you?"

Was it a little goodwill gesture? Then, silently Mr. Owl took wing in the direction of a distant tree grove, more than likely to snooze. Thank goodness this time he didn't leave breakfast!

Mr. Owl still perches from time to time in our trees with a wink and a "hoo, hoo, how are you?" We just wish he was more fastidious.

Chapter Ten
↓
Backyard Tales II: Protective Parents

"Look at me! Look at me! Look at me!"

A brown/rust/black/white fluff ball races past me while I walk across our yard. The adorable big-eyed chick seems to be showing off. His black necklaced siblings soon take chase. Soon, a loud alarm call is heard – "Kill Dee, Kill Dee, Kill Dee—stop, drop, freeze and hide!" the parent warns.

Nothing is more protective than a killdeer parent. Who doesn't admire them?

These graceful birds arrive in early spring. We have witnessed them court and set up housekeeping. This spring was no exception. How blessed we feel to be a part of their world every year.

"We will build a life together and raise our young" the male says to his mate. They always share tasks and responsibilities.

And so it begins. First they work on their home which is quite modest, only a depression in pebbles.

But, look again. It is all camouflage. Little by little, they furnish their simple abode much like humans, one piece at a time until it is comfortable. Pebbles and other materials must match so predators are fooled. It is simply amazing what these little builders create.

Yet, if a large animal like a cow or horse come too close the parent will fluff up, put their tail feathers over their head and run at the huge animal. They are selfless when it comes to their young. I witnessed this in our pasture. It works! The cow or horse has no interest in the eggs. But, one hoof means total destruction of a nest. Killdeer are vigilant and unyielding.

One spring we had to put a saw-horse in our driveway so vehicles would not drive over the little hidden home of a killdeer. It was too well camouflaged.

I recall a particularly stormy spring night. The wind was vicious and the rain came pelting down in torrents. Lightening zigzagged across the sky while thunder boomed. After a while tiny streams flowed in our gravel driveway. It looked hopeless for the brave Killdeer siting on her nest. The nest could be seen from our front door. My heart went out to the brave little bird.

She never flinched or fled. Instead, she remained steadfast throughout the ordeal. Her little head would turn from time to time as if to say, "Oh, please. I am tired and wet. If only the wind and rain would stop. I am worried about my babies."

"Peep, peep, peep, peep, peep" the babies could be heard inside their eggshells.

"Oh, my precious babies I am here. So is your Daddy. We are here. We will keep you safe. The wind and rain will soon be gone and the sun will come out tomorrow. Go back to sleep little ones," the mother softly said.

Being a young mother, this was her first experience with such a violent storm. Her mate was nearby. Soon he would take her place on the nest. He was a very dependable mate and shared parenting duties.

The sun shone brightly the next morning, albeit the earth was saturated. Soon the day grew warm and mellow with promise. I looked out my window and did not see the killdeer. I hoped they were not washed away in the deluge.

Walking out later to get the mail I heard shrill little calls. Not far from the driveway I noticed three little fluff balls racing in the grass. Killdeer chicks were alive and full of mischief. They delighted me! They were ready to roll the moment they opened their big eyes and dried off. I was grateful they made it through the wretched storm. I was overjoyed for the little bird family.

"You can't catch me, can't catch me, can't catch me," they cried out cheerfully.

I remember how hard it was to resist getting closer to the pretty little chicks. However, their protective parents immediately took charge of the situation. Faking injury, the mother bird dropped a wing. She pretended it was broken. Oh yes, she was tempting me to follow her. It's a ploy that usually works. I admired her beauty and courage. I played along with her. Every now and then she would slow down, turn and look my way. Eventually, she stopped. When she noticed her chicks were safely hidden she quickly flew off with a mocking "Kill Dee, Kill Dee!"

Whether it was dangerous weather or a dangerous predator, the parents never gave a second thought to their own comfort or safety.

We feel the proud parents like to parade their young for us. Do they sense our admiration? Perhaps, who knows? At times they seem to boast or show off their handsome little ones while we grill on the patio. They "show and tell" not just for us, but for other birds as well. It is always entertaining to see them sprint or race by.

We also hear the night call of their parents, "It's time to bed down for the night. It is time to sleep, time to sleep, time to hide and sleep."

I always worry about little birds if a parent's call is heard after dark. I recognize the desperate plea of a parent in their warning calls. "Curfew, curfew, curfew. It's very late, where are you?"

I recall a regal goose family that nested not far from our front door. They waddled across the backyard with their goslings in a sort of "Sunday

School parade." It was enduring. It looked like a fairy tale. First father goose, four goslings, and taking up the rear, mother goose. Sadly, tragedy struck. A predator or predators wiped out all but one youngster. We felt sorrow for the goose parents. No wonder the shrill call of the little killdeer always causes me concern. What chance would their young have if goslings are taken so easily? Like human beings, animal parents do their best. Nevertheless, through no fault of their own, outside forces can take their young away. Nature can be cruel and unforgiving.

Lessons must be learned.

"This is a survival skill you will need when I am no longer with you. This is what you should eat. This is where to hide. This is a dangerous place. This is a safe place. This is the proper way to take off and land," the killdeer preaches to their young.

The killdeer never stopped teaching their little ones many valuable lessons all summer. I will miss their loud calls and flight displays when they migrate. Yet, I know they will return next season and bring their energy and glee. A much better name for killdeer is Joy. For that is what they give us time and time again, Joy!

"*The gypsies believe the bear to be a brother to man because he has the same body beneath his hide, because he drinks beer, because he enjoys music and because he likes to dance.*"

—Hemingway

CHAPTER ELEVEN

TWO CUBS

YELLOWSTONE 1955

"Daddy, look at the brown bear. He is walking towards us," I said in my five-year-old voice.

Quickly, my dad took my hand, looked down at me and said. "We are going to walk slowly Hoppy. We need to get back to the car. See Kevin and Mommy are already inside."

I recall my mother's anxious expression and my older brother's bewildered glance. More than likely they were both wondering what was taking us so long. But, my dad and I were taken with the whole majesty of Yellowstone with its tall lodge pole pine, Douglas fir and spruce trees. The scent was glorious. The day before I complained about the smelly, sulphur smell of the mud pots. The wooden walkway terrified me, but my mother held my hand tightly the whole time. She kept me safe and was very cautious of the dangerous springs. The brightly colored mud and strangeness of it all frightened me, however. The steam venting and boiling mud looked otherworldly. No place on earth compares to Yellowstone for its variety of springs, geysers and wildlife. It is enchanting and mysterious.

Now, my dad had reason to pick up our pace. A young brown bear was headed for us at a clip. His cinnamon brown fur thrilled me. He looked like my teddy bear back home. I loved my teddy, a Christmas gift from a couple years past. We would dance together for hours spinning and twirling about. Sometimes he would sip tea with me. I preferred his company to the prissy dolls. As little girl I seldom played with dolls. But, I adored my brown teddy. I still have him after sixty years. Well, the brown bear cub was the same color. But, this fellow was no toy, nor was he a little cub. He no longer needed his mother to care for him. He was on his own. Perhaps he was over two or three. Like so many bears, he was an opportunist. More than likely he enjoyed picnic leftovers or had grown accustomed to tourists tossing tidbits to him. Still, to me he was adorable. Never mind his size or strength.

In seconds the bear was by my side. He walked with me, like a dog heeling. Every now and then he would glance up with what appeared a bear smile. To me animals communicated like people. They either smiled or frowned, laughed or cried. So, it made sense the bear simply wanted to be friends. For some reason the young bear had no interest in my dad. Surprisingly, he had no interest in what remained of our picnic lunch which was hastily abandoned on the table. His focus was directed on me. I was charmed.

"Do not pet him Hoppy. Keep your hands to yourself. He is wild. Just walk with me back to the car," my daddy warned.

No, he was not Smokey the Bear, Winnie the Pooh, or my little brown teddy bear. Yet, when the bear walked alongside me I noticed he seemed playful, like a big furry dog. His demeanor in no way seemed threatening.

Now I was taught the Ten Commandments at an early age. The 5th Commandment is: Honor thy Father and Mother. So, why did I disobey and put my hand on the bear's shoulder? I could not resist touching him because we were pals, or so I thought.

The big cub's coat was thick and coarse. My tiny fingers sunk deeply into his cinnamon coat. I noticed his wild smell was nothing like my teddy back home. It was a thrilling experience to feel the wild animal and see him look into my eyes. But, it was not to last long. For within seconds the cub placed himself in front of us, took my left leg in both paws and gently started to swing it back and forth. Then he got a little rougher and swung with more force. My red corduroy pants were shredded. I was frozen. My dad scooped me up. I recall shrieking in fear. When we reached the car, the door flew open, I was tossed inside, the door slammed shut and we sped off to the Ranger station. The frolicking bear thought it was some sort of game because he rolled alongside my racing dad, which terrified us both. My poor mother by now was beside herself. Looking back, it must have been a nightmare for her watching the scene unfold.

When we sat in the ranger station I felt ashamed but relieved. My child's heart knew I disobeyed my father's warning. Looking down I noticed a lot of blood was running down my leg. It was beginning to hurt a lot as well. Yet, I was embarrassed more that my nice corduroy pants were in tatters. They were a badge of disobedience.

The kind park ranger applied first aid and dressing while my mother assisted him. The wounds were not serious and no stitches were required. But my parents were alarmed by the incident. I felt certain I ruined their Yellowstone adventure.

"More than likely the bear thought she was another cub. He was playing with her. Believe me, if he wasn't the leg would be far worse. Yes, the bear felt she was a playmate. We will move the bear to another area," the ranger said. I was very happy the bear cub would not be punished or harmed. He was only trying to have fun.

When we got back to the hotel I remember my mother hugging me and asking "Why didn't you listen?" I learned a life-long lesson in respect. Obey your parents and obey your elders. For no matter how old I got, their sage advice was never off track. Some lessons were hard ones, but nothing compared to my bear encounter. The brown bear cub left an indelible mark on me.

"Until one loves an animal,
a part of one's soul remains unawakened"
—Anatole France

I come to the garden alone
While the dew is still on the roses.
And the voice I hear,
falling on my ear,
The Son of God discloses.
And He walks with me,
And he talks with me,
And He tells me I am His own.
And the joy we share as we tarry there
None other has ever known.

—C. Austin Miles
1912

CHAPTER TWELVE
ᚤ ᚤ
THE HUMMINGBIRD

Hummingbird

The sunlight speaks. And its voice is a bird:
It glitters half-guessed half seen half heard
Above the flower bed. Over the lawn:
A flashing dip and it is gone.
And all it lends to the eye is this—
A sunbeam giving the air a kiss.

—Harry Kemp

It was late summer when the once-vibrant flowers started to lose their bloom—a transitory time. It is a bittersweet passage in nature before the burnt oranges and deep russet hues show off their brilliant jewels. Soft muted pinks, blues, and yellows are replaced with spice hues of garnet or gold. Mums of coral or copper are opulent to behold. Soon it would be their time. And so early September is often summer's last visage of bygone days, filled with pastel beauty and grace. These were the last glorious days to celebrate.

Kristi was working in her garden that day. The sun cast a warm golden glow that afternoon. The air was clean and crisp with only a slight peaceful breeze. Cottonball clouds floated lazily across an azure sky while gossamer winged butterflies performed ballets. She was determined to gather as many of the sumptuous flowers as she could before they began to fade. It was no small task given the size of her massive country garden. Her love of flowers created a sort of Eden, filled with all colors and varieties. It was a fantastic garden, one only devotion and love creates.

A few hours passed and she realized it was time to get lunch prepared for herself and husband, Kim. They would have a light lunch on the patio rather than inside, a little picnic for two. Leaving her garden gloves, shears, and clogs by the back doorstep, she noticed something iridescent quickly flash in the back of the garage.

As she took a second glance she was horrified. A frantic hummingbird was trying to free itself from a huge orb weaver web. The tiny metallic acrobat was no match for the three-foot concentric construction. The almost invisible web had gone unnoticed the night before in the large garage. The nocturnal spider's lacy handiwork was impressive. During the day the spider would lay in wait to snare unsuspecting prey, in this case the terrified hummingbird.

It would not be long before the vulnerable little visitor would be encased and wrapped by the orange-brown bulbous spider. What a dreadful end. Now a hummingbird can fly right, left, up, down, backwards, upside down, even in a figure eight. Their exquisite wings flap around eighty times per second. But, they are vulnerable to all kinds of enemies from climate change, people, feral cats, pesticides other birds, and insects.

The search for nectar or perhaps the web itself drew the hapless creature into the maze. Hummingbirds use spider webs in their nest construction. The webs stretch to accommodate the growth of young birds. They are diminutive geniuses. But, this was highly unlikely given it was not the breeding season. Indeed, it was late summer. No, it was not the web itself. The tiny bird was captivated by the many fragrant flowers sitting in containers to be later placed throughout the house. The garage resembled a flower market!

Acting swiftly, Kristi placed her garden gloves back on. With deft hands she ever so gently cupped the tiny prisoner. She delicately pulled the webs from the hummingbird, first the long tapered beak, then face, wings and feet. The bird fluttered in fear but within seconds sensed she was safe.

"Don't worry, you are free little beauty," she said softly. It was a rare moment to behold between the human and her little winged visitor.

The exquisite feathered creature began to revive from the grip of its nightmare. Still tenderly cupped on its back, the bird studied the face of her rescuer with furtive glances. Then, she straightened her beautiful glistening body, spread her fine wings and gracefully sped away. The wee bird seemed to glitter away rather than fly. Kristi was held spellbound, captivated by what just took place.

She curiously followed the hummingbird's path. It led around to the patio where her husband Kim had been reading tranquilly in a lounge chair. It was a perfect place for a sojourn. The soft breeze and lovely fragrant flowers lulled him to sweet sleep.

Suddenly, she spotted the rescued hummingbird. Rather than hover around the flower garden or potted plants, she softly, effortlessly rested on Kim's forehead for a few minutes.

"What in the world is going on?" Kristi thought to herself. It was a beguiling moment.

For in early spring, Kim had been diagnosed with brain cancer and had undergone surgery. Like the hummingbird, he too bravely struggled with the insidious spider web of cancer and found himself struggling to free himself from its evil grasp.

The beautiful little bird sat so demurely that Kim never felt it land or leave. It was more like a fairy kiss. It was a moment of pure enchantment for Kristi to witness. She was awestruck.

Kim lived for over a decade after his surgery.

Tragically, much like the orb weaver spider, cancer lays in wait and strikes when we often least expect it.

I believe, in its little otherworldly way, the glittering hummingbird somehow tried to free Kim out of gratitude for being rescued by Kristi. Perhaps it was a blessing from a winged messenger? Who knows? By all accounts it was amazing, just like Kim.

"Hope is the thing with feathers."
—Emily Dickinson

Chapter Thirteen
⚕ ⚕
Sparkman
Location, Location, Location!

Walking through a country gift store years ago, I spotted a handmade birdhouse. It was crafted out of repurposed cedar and painted a distressed red. It was unique and sweet, with much detail. In fact it resembled a miniature firehouse complete with tiny bell, hose and pail. It was charming. What made it even more adorable was the working wee bell which hung outside the bird hole. Over the door in whimsical lettering was written the word Sparkman. I couldn't resist it.

When I got home, I hung it outside our front door which faced east. The covered front porch sheltered the birdhouse from inclement weather and the morning sun gently caressed the doorway. Our little cabin-like home had vines growing down the porch posts and railings giving it a hidden-hideaway feel. The rustic, wooden birdhouse complimented the exterior perfectly. It's funny how simple things like the birdhouse bring joy.

At the time we lived in a small town. My husband worked just a few blocks away so he usually ate lunch at home. It was his daily routine.

Within a week of placing the little birdhouse by our entryway, we noticed a male house wren checking it out. "Must be prime real estate!" I said, laughing.

When my husband came home the next day for lunch, he noticed something unique. Just as he stepped inside the front door, the house wren hopped out of the Sparkman firehouse and rang the tiny bell "ding, ding, ding, ding!" Then, the little bird stretched his neck out and sang at the top of his teensy lungs. It was startling!

After his mini-concert he hopped back inside the little firehouse. We were delighted by his antics. Day after day the wren rang the miniature bell accompanied by his boisterous songs. Some of our neighbors noticed the little bird's behavior too. It was sheer entertainment for everybody.

Indeed, the house wren truly was the Sparkman because many admiring females were drawn to his "sparking and courting" style. He had a lot of swagger for such a wee bird—a real rock star of the wren world.

Our little birdhouse weathered many storms and sheltered many little bird families over the years. We put up many pretty and unique birdhouses along fences, trees and porches. But, none captivated birds quite so much as that one. It held a special magic.

We still have the birdhouse although it needs repairs. The whimsical Sparkman lettering still remains intact. Yet, the little roof is leaking and the bell was completely worn out. We plan on placing it up once again for a new homeowner. But we doubt it will ever house one like the musical genius in the guise of a house wren named Sparkman.

Prayer for
the Animals

Hear our humble prayer, O God,
for our friends, the animals,
especially for animals who are suffering,
for any that are hunted or lost
or deserted or frightened or hungry,
for all that must be put to death.

We entreat for them all Thy mercy and pity,
and for those who deal with them,
we ask a heart of compassion and gentle hands
and kindly words.

Make us, ourselves, to be true friends to animals,
and so to share the blessings of the merciful.

— *Albert Schweitzer*

MEMORY LANE

"To live in hearts we leave behind is not to die."
— Thomas Campbell

<u>NAME</u> <u>YOUR SPECIAL FRIEND</u>

Aaron	Bentley (dog)
Autumn	Angel (cat)
Bev	Trax (horse)
Bria	Cricket (dog)
Carol J.	Marco Polo & Buffy (dog & cat)
Carol M.	Callie & Chief (dog & cat)

Cathleen	Oakie & Squeak (dog & cat)
Cheryl	Jazzy (cat)
Claudia	Goldie (dog)
D.E.	Scout (dog)
Gail	Ricky (dog)
Grace	Putison (cat)
Irene	Bingo (bird)
Jay & Jeremy	Beau (dog)
Jennifer	Kayla (dog)
John	Ramona (cow)
Maggie	Smokey (cat)
Marie	Sugar (bird)
Steve	Tippy (dog)
Tara	Max & Storm (dog & cat)
Terry	Chief & Thor (dogs)
Theresa	Simon (cat)
Todd	Nathan (horse)

Please add <u>Your</u> Special Friend to this list!

_____   _____

YOUR NAME   YOUR SPECIAL FRIEND

Thurs Oct 1, 1953

Maple Lake, Ill.

ABOUT THE AUTHOR

Carol Blackford is also the author of *Grateful Heart, A True Story of Faith, Hope and Love*. A Sioux Falls native, she always wanted to teach. Her first calling was to become a Kindergarten teacher, but instead taught 9-12 high school English. However, that was not to last. In 1981 she found herself teaching college English for South Dakota State University as well as other area colleges and universities.

She shares her little country home with her husband Terry. She states, "I always find inspiration in this simple, sweet place."

Carol can be reached at:
travthepaint@gmail.com

Grateful Heart

Carol Blackford's first book, *Grateful Heart: A True Story of Faith, Hope and Love,* was published in 2015. It has earned high praise from readers on Amazon and Goodreads.

> "She is an impeccable wordsmith.
> Ms. Blackford provides a gentle road map,"

> "If everyone could have their
> story told like this."

> "Divine interventions do exist! I can't wait
> for the next Carol Blackford book!"

Grateful Heart is available in select bookstores, as well as Amazon and Goodreads stores online.